D0505128

NLP
Counselling

Roy Bailey

DEDICATION

To Felicity, Fraser, Mum, Dad and Shirley,
and the fond memory of my dear brother Hughie

HELPING PEOPLE CHANGE:
THE ESSENTIAL
COUNSELLING SERIES

NLP
Counselling

Roy Bailey

Speechmark Publishing Ltd
Telford Road, Bicester, Oxon OX26 4LQ, UK

Published by
Speechmark Publishing Ltd, Telford Road, Bicester, Oxon OX26 4LQ, United
Kingdom
www.speechmark.net

First published 1997
Reprinted 2001

Typeset by Applecart, Bicester, Oxon

002-2287/Printed in Great Britain/2000

British Library Cataloguing in Publication Data
Bailey, Roy
  NLP Counselling
  1. Neurolinguistic programming 2. Counselling
  1. Title
  158.3

ISBN 0 86388 345 1
(Previously published by Winslow Press Ltd under ISBN 0 86388 157 2)

CONTENTS

Roy Bailey is a chartered clinical and counselling psychologist, hypnotherapist, counsellor, psychotherapist and training consultant. He is the founding Principal of the Centre for Personal Excellence, a human services organization committed to improving individual health and well-being and promoting personal excellence through applied counselling psychology. He is also the co-founder of the Lifestyle Management Systems concept and Lifestyle Information Stress Analysis (LISA) system.

Roy is the author and seminar leader of many stress management and counselling workshops, as well as the originator of the 'Practical Counselling Skills', 'Personal Empowerment Training' and 'CrisisCare' training programmes. He is the editor of *Helping People Change: The Essential Counselling Series*. His other books and publications include *Practical Counselling Skills, 50 Activities for Managing Stress, 50 Activities for Developing Counselling Skills, How to Identify and Manage Stress, Coping with Stress in Caring, Stress and Coping in Nursing, Systematic Relaxation, Personal Influence and Assertiveness, CrisisCare, How to Empower People at Work, LISA – Lifestyle Information Stress Analysis* and *Personal Empowerment Strategies.*

PREFACE TO THE SERIES

Welcome to *Helping People Change: the Essential Counselling Series*. Counselling skills are now becoming more and more recognized as an essential part of effective helping. Nowhere is this more true than in social services, education, the health care professions and their associates. In publishing this series Winslow has produced a range of books on different approaches to counselling that should be of immediate practical benefit to anyone in the 'people business'. Each book in the series is written by experienced counsellors respected in their own field. Each title reveals a different way in which you can develop your counselling skills with your clients. I hope you will find them a welcome and close companion in your work.

ROY BAILEY
Series Editor

Note: Many of the case examples in this book are derived from practical counselling sessions. The real identities of these cases have been removed and examples changed in the interests of protecting the clients.

ACKNOWLEDGEMENTS

I should like to thank Michael Mott for his collaboration in conceiving some of the ideas in this book. I have kept the plural pronoun in much of the book because of my appreciation of his contribution to my thinking in the early life of the book. Thanks also to Catherine McAllister, Sue Christelow and the rest of the Winslow team in creating this book; and to Ian Franklin for a superb cover design. I am grateful to Stephen Brooks for the use of the 'kicking feet' example.

My most prominent influences have been Carl Rogers, Milton Erickson, Bob Wubbolding, Will Schutz, Richard Bandler, Richard Lazarus and, more recently, Stephen Brooks and Paul Watzlawick. I would also like to credit all the other therapists, counsellors and clients who have helped me over the years to formulate my ideas on counselling with NLP.

Lest I forget: special thanks to my clients and all my colleagues now using NLP in counselling.

Chapter 1

COUNSELLING WITH NEUROLINGUISTIC PROGRAMMING

NLP: a Metaphor for Counselling

●

This book is about counselling with Neurolinguistic Programming — NLP counselling for short. Counselling with NLP involves working on many levels with clients. You may find it useful to think about the NLP counselling process as like going up and down in an elevator in a multi-storey building. First of all the client and the counsellor need to get into the lift together. They then find out where the lift buttons are and which ones they want to press. Now they are ready to travel on many journeys.

The client and the counsellor then start to find out what is on each floor. When they can do this they can venture out of the lift and explore and discover what is there and whether or not they want to stay there or go back in the lift. They can travel to well-known floors and remind themselves of the familiar surroundings. They can visit levels they have never been on before and be curious about what they might learn. They can keep returning to the same floor. They can pause between floors. They can spend more time on one floor than another or flit from floor to floor, scanning what is on each level before choosing to do something else. Deciding to participate in the counselling process — to be in or out of the lift — is worked out between the counsellor and the client. One of the first discoveries is finding out what the client's favourite lift buttons are controlling and which levels they will take them to. They may prefer to stay at ground level or automatically go into the basement each time. Some may prefer to shoot right up to the top floor and look out and see the view that lies ahead.

The more they visit the different floors, the more they can experience what is on them. For some clients these experiences are ones which they may wish to repeat often. For others one experience may be enough for them to learn about one specific part of the building they need to inhabit. Others again will choose to have many experiences and many ways of changing their experiences. It all depends on how they experience the journey and what is going on at different stops along the way. When they are able to utilize what is on each of their levels, they can choose the experiences they would like to have and the way to have them. The counsellor's task is to help the client control the elevator.

NLP Counselling and the Counselling Process

●

The associations and similarities between the elevator metaphor and mainstream counselling are many and clear. In counselling with NLP we create core conditions for change. We create rapport. We reflect, match and mirror what the client is doing, saying and feeling. We cultivate respect. We express and communicate empathy to clients. We listen and provide a climate of caring that creates conditions for client change. Genuineness and positive regard are utilized by the counsellor. The client is enabled to discover the personal information that allows them to feel, see and hear what they are thinking and doing. Conscious and unconscious levels of the client's experience are examined. Specific problems and general lifestyle choices are made.

Habits, challenges, choices and changes are all part of NLP counselling. It is concerned with valuing, accepting and confronting clients. Trust is at its core. Trust is the cement which holds together everything the NLP counsellor does with the client. The process of NLP counselling enables clients to explore, understand and take action in significant areas of their lives. Clearly the process and the skills used by counsellors in NLP counselling are similar in many ways to those of mainstream person-centred counselling — not the same, but similar. NLP counselling is also very different.

A Task for the Reader
●

We have a number of tasks for you. As you read this book you will notice and learn about further similarities and differences between NLP counselling and the kinds of counselling you may practise at present. Whether you are new to or experienced in counselling or NLP, you may be curious about the way NLP counselling can be usefully integrated into your work with clients. You may also be interested in the way NLP counselling works and the way it is used with the various clients described in this book. First of all, however, we would like you to be curious about NLP itself.

The Origins of Neurolinguistic Programming
●

What is Neurolinguistic Programming and how did it come about? Let us begin by being clear about what we mean. Neurolinguistic Programming is difficult to say easily and elegantly. 'Neuro' is derived from the Greek 'neuron' meaning 'nerve', and in NLP refers to the assumption that all behaviour is the result of neurological processes. 'Linguistic' is also a derivation, this time from the Latin 'lingua', the root of our word 'language'. The linguistic part of NLP stands for the principle that neural processes are ordered, organized and dynamically formulated into personal models and strategies which are represented through language and systems of communication. Finally, 'Programming' refers to the processes used by human beings in organizing and reorganizing their sensory representations of their world in order to achieve specific outcomes. Programming also produces behaviours we call strategies. It is these personal neurolinguistic strategies and behaviours which the NLP counsellor and client work with in counselling. We believe that the purpose of NLP counselling is to enable clients to model strategies that result in satisfying their personal outcomes for their lives.

It is generally acknowledged that John Grinder and Richard Bandler were the founding fathers of NLP. John Grinder, a professor of linguistics at the University of California, and Richard Bandler, a student at the university with an interest in psychotherapy and computers, collaborated in studying leading therapists. Amongst other things they were particularly interested in and curious about the patterns (see pages 6-7) used by outstanding psychotherapists and counsellors. The three main therapists they studied were Fritz Perls, Virginia Satir and Milton Erickson. Perls was regarded as an innovative therapist and the leading protagonist of the Gestalt school of therapy. Satir had an extraordinary reputation for her outstanding work with families. She seemed to be able to help families resolve apparently insoluble problems and change family relationships in a way which other therapists found impossible. The final therapist they studied was Milton Erickson — lately regarded by many as the world's leading psychohypnotherapist and guru of modern hypnotherapy. Erickson, Satir and Perls brought profound changes in their clients, often in a very few sessions and even in a few moments of therapy.

Grinder and Bandler discovered and analysed the patterns of these highly effective therapists. As personalities the latter were very different. As therapists they used a similar range of patterns in their work with clients and patients. These patterns were identifiable, analysable and could be grouped into specific structures used by each of the therapists. Depending on the client and the particular therapist or counsellor, a different emphasis on one or more neurolinguistic patterns could be utilized in counselling and psychotherapy.

These discoveries encompassed the language used by therapists with their clients. They also involved the neural patterns that underpinned the language used in therapy and the way in which reality was sensorily represented in experience and programmed and expressed as behaviour. Neurolinguistic Programming was born. The implications for counselling, psychotherapy, hypnotherapy and practising therapists were enormous. Therapists found they could learn to replicate the patterns of Erickson, Satir and Perls. Once they knew the model of effective therapy they could reproduce it themselves and in turn become great NLP counsellors and psychotherapists.

Neurolinguistic Programming: a Model for Counselling
●

We believe that Neurolinguistic Programming provides a practical model for counselling. For us NLP counselling is the discipline whose domain encompasses the structure and dynamics of subjective experience. NLP counselling has no affiliations with any theory. In fact NLP counselling is not a theory. When we are counselling with NLP we are therefore not concerned about whether what we are doing is true or false. In NLP counselling we are interested only in whether or not what we have done and how it has been done is useful. In this sense NLP counselling has the status of a model. Our model in NLP counselling is simply charged with providing a description of how something works. Thus NLP counselling is either useful or not useful. The term 'model' in NLP counselling is something which sets it apart from 'theories' of counselling.

Counsellors using NLP are therefore modellers. If they have a good model it will be useful at a particular time. If not, they need to discover and describe another model. As Carlyle was reputed to have said, "Show me a model and I will tell you if it works." Counselling with NLP involves tracing, mapping, organizing and reorganizing the client's and counsellor's models of the world: how human beings model and experience the world in which they live. Therefore counselling with NLP is not only different from theories of counselling, it is different from other models of psychology and behaviour. NLP in counselling is a meta-model.

NLP Counselling Procedures and Skills

●

Counselling with NLP also involves utilizing a set of procedures and skills in our interactions with others whom, in the context of counselling, we call clients. Usefulness is the criterion by which we judge the efficacy of NLP counselling. NLP counselling offers counsellors a specific range of techniques. Using them a counsellor may organize or reorganize their own subjective experiences or the experiences of a client. The purpose of this activity is to define satisfactorily and subsequently realize a behavioural outcome. There are therefore three fundamental questions NLP counsellors ask themselves when working with clients: Has what we have been doing been useful? How did we do it? What was the outcome?

The Importance of Patterning

●

As well as modelling, NLP counselling is distinguished from other forms of counselling by the importance of *patterning*. Essentially, patterning in NLP accounts for the particular cognitions and behaviours each individual produces as a result of the way they represent their experience. Patterning has three main characteristics in counselling with NLP. First of all patterns are dynamically created by each client describing them for those counsellors who may be initiating or responding to the pattern being described and their possible responses and actions. Many patterns are then the basis of valued generalizations about the world of the client and are more or less well formed in their structure. A second characteristic of patterning in counselling with NLP is that client descriptions are represented through the sensory systems accessible to the client. The main sensory systems are visual, auditory, kinaesthetic and olfactory. The focus on the client emphasizes that NLP counselling is user-based. In this NLP counselling is not unlike the person-centred counselling of Carl Rogers, but this similarity apart, they are very different. Client patterns represented in sensory terms are idiosyncratic to each client. By definition client patterns are individual. They are specific to the client and contain a multitude of representations arising from the sensory capabilities available to each client. A third characteristic of counselling with NLP is that its descriptive vocabulary includes references to feelings, thoughts and body processes which are not directly observable to the counsellor or the client.

Cognitions in NLP Counselling
●

The individual cognitions and behaviours that clients and counsellors bring to counselling are the programmed results of dynamic and structured combinations that have been sequenced and organized into their neural systems. These personal cognitions and behaviours are appraised against valued criteria and sensorily represented in the sights, sounds, feelings, smells and tastes of people and the way they speak and act in different situations. They also underpin the patterns, rapport, decisions, choices, flexibility and information which NLP counsellors utilize in counselling. Personal cognitions and behaviour are fundamental in understanding clients and their problems and in promoting client change.

A Personal Cognitive–Behavioural Model for Counselling with NLP
●

We have found it useful to adopt a person-focused approach to NLP counselling which also permits the application of NLP technology with clients. Our practical model for NLP counselling (Figure 1) is cognitive–behavioural in its assumptions and based on the work of the psychologists Richard Lazarus and Roy Bailey.

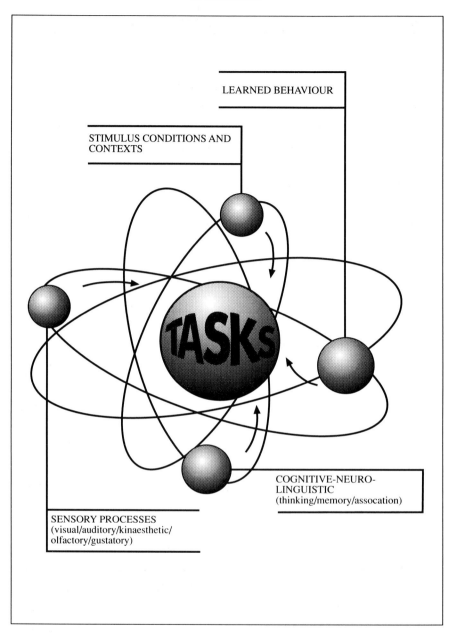

Figure 1 *A personal cognitive–behavioural model*

Personal Appraisals in NLP Counselling

●

The approach in this model is personal because it is the client's own individual and often highly idiosyncratic sensory–cognitive appraisals of the internal and external demands they perceive as being made upon them which are the critical factors in the way they experience reality. The following is an example of these personal appraisals. One retired couple that came for counselling had argued a great deal since the retirement of the husband. A counsellor worked with them and discovered that many of the rows that came about were brought on by the rattling and banging sounds from their old washing machine. The husband, who had retired six months earlier, found that 'the incessant droning and banging' from the machine got on his nerves and was extremely aggravating. It reminded him of the air raids over London during the Second World War and how he used to get very angry having to put up with the noise night after night. His solution to the rows with his wife was to spend some of his retirement nest egg on a new state-of-the-art hi-tech combined washing machine and tumble dryer and surprise her with it as a retirement gift. The wife had a very different experience. She was fond of 'the good old reliable machine'. She found the sounds very 'comforting and reassuring' and that the noise was more a rhythmical background she had heard for many years and one which reminded her of all the ups and downs in her marriage — and yet her marriage had managed to continue working despite other marriages breaking down and people changing their partners and seeking new relationships. Her solution was to keep the machine and keep it going for as long as she possibly could. She was adamant she would not replace it — at almost any cost.

Here we clearly have two very different perceptions and appraisals of an objectively agreed situation, and also very different solutions. In the words of the songwriter, Nillson, 'you hear what you want to hear and you see what you want to see — you dig?' Interestingly the cognitive–behavioural model of counselling is also flexible enough to account for the clients in the example changing their minds. Further personal appraisal may change their experience as the external situation changes or as they change their perceptions of an unchanged external situation. In our example one way change may have come about was through changing the machine, the other through changing their minds about keeping it. Clearly it all depended on what they thought of the rattling and banging of the machine.

Client Cognitions in NLP Counselling

●

Cognition is another important aspect of our counselling model. We believe that language, thinking, memory and association, and the psycholinguistic meaning or personal significance of internal and external events are the central psychological mediators in determining our personal experience.

Why is this such a useful part of our model of counselling? One of the first things it does is provide us with answers to the fundamental issues of 'cause' that need to be tackled in counselling clients: every problem clients bring to counselling need not always be produced by the same causes; and the same apparent causes can produce different problems. Cognition also accounts for the many meanings attached to and the various ways by which clients resolve their personal difficulties.

The personal–cognitive–behavioural (PCB) model of counselling accounts for 'the mystery of the first mediator'. In our view the first mediator is cognitive. It is cognition that accounts for the meanings clients give to their problems, personalities and the way they perceive themselves. It is cognition which clients use as best they know how to make sense of their own behaviour and the behaviour of others. Cognition influences behaviour and behaviour influences cognition. However it is the personal cognitions of clients which matter in NLP counselling. Changes in personal cognition are the motivators for client behavioural change in NLP counselling. We find that personal cognitions can also be the barrier to change in counselling and cause the perpetuation of perceived problems by clients. Therefore we argue that personal cognition is the gateway through which NLP counsellors build rapport; they understand and facilitate the process of change with and through their clients.

Our personal–cognitive–behavioural model of counselling is a psychological model and one which is consistent with the findings of Wolf and Goodall's (1968) study of patients: 'Man is vulnerable because he reacts not only to the actual existence of danger, but to threats and symbols of danger experienced in his past.' (page 3).

This model is tremendously useful for counsellors and clients. It accounts for the way each client engages in thinking about their problems and the situations they find fearful, stressful, worrying or confusing and incapacitating. It also makes clear that language, memory, association and the meaning clients attribute to events in their lives and the values they put on them can be understood within a person-oriented counselling process. The cognitive part of our model accounts for the client who thinks their life has been a productive struggle with all its painful memories as well as the one who thinks their life has been a purposeless waste of time and energy. The personal significance of thinking, memory and the associations clients have with it are central to the work we do with clients in NLP counselling. In our experience, the range and content of client cognitions can be concerned with the past, present and the future. So, for example, in counselling we can ask clients not only to recall the past but to say what they think they may have learned from the past that they can use to change their situation today or in the future.

Clients, Cognitive Behaviour and Personal Significance
●

In NLP counselling, clients' behaviour includes the way they think, the way they say they feel, their associations and their memories. In NLP counselling client behaviour is the cause and the result of personal cognitions. It accounts for the way clients think about themselves, what is going on inside them and the way they represent their so-called external world of realities in observable or inferable behaviour. NLP counselling is a cyclical process informed through the feedback of information that is regarded as personally significant to each client.

As we see it, it is the personal meaning client behaviours have for clients which are of central interest to NLP counsellors and the counselling process. Each counselling session has a personal significance for clients and counsellors. The personal significance of events affects the degree of stress experienced by clients and the extent to which they believe they are capable of coping with crises and difficulties they face. Our model assumes that cognitive appraisals are made continuously by clients as a way of monitoring their internal and external environments. These appraisals may be fast, automatic and habitual, so that they are outside the awareness of clients — in our experience most of them are. However clients may also make deliberate attempts to 'weigh up' events in their lives in a way which they are more conscious of doing. This is a complex issue that requires a fuller discussion. However, for our perspective on NLP counselling, it should suffice to say that client cognitive appraisals can range from being fast, continuous and automatic to slow, intermittent and deliberate.

Essentially the purpose of client cognitive appraisals is to provide feedback. Why is this feedback so important? In short, feedback provides clients with information which is then evaluated for its degree of personal threat, harm or potential loss. Clients who perceive a significant degree of threat, harm or loss are then mobilized into behaving in the best way they can to cope with their perceived difficulties. In this counselling model clients may also perceive and appraise their internal or external environments as benign or challenging. In such cases they may not be inclined to seek counselling, unless of course they find they are bored and frustrated with the routine and regularity of their predictable personal lives.

However it is people who are in pain or at least some degree of distress who most frequently become clients in counselling. One person facing a simple operation involving minor surgery may think they are 'very fortunate to get the operation' and look forward to it in a trusting manner and relaxed mood, while another about to have the same operation may appraise the prospect in such a way that the personal significance of the event is experienced as terrifying. In such a case the individual may have regarded the prospective operation as 'harmful' and subsequently experienced anxiety.

Even the most harrowing of traumatic events can be cognitively appraised by clients in different ways. Their personal significance may allow them to cope more or less well with the crisis they are experiencing. In a recent example, someone who had undergone a traumatic experience seemed to cope very well under extraordinarily demanding circumstances:

> ... a recent victim of a car bomb suffered severe injuries to both legs. However, he appraised the situation as one with which he could cope, since he was physically fit, highly trained and his morale was good. Later he attributed his survival to this appraisal.
>
> Bailey and Clarke, 1989

Harmless Circumstances
●

Our personal–cognitive–behavioural model of counselling does something else that many other models of counselling and psychology do not. It shows us how clients can be upset, experience stress, be terrified or feel helpless to cope with circumstances that are apparently harmless to most others: benign matters such as the colour red, blue or green; the angle at which a person folds their arms; a white coffee cup; a book torn on its front cover; cracks in the pavement; a white furry rabbit; a magnificent horse; cats; dogs; the way a person smiles or says their name; the sound of a train passing in the night; the dark; feeling the weight of another person's body; the touch of a hand; the smell of perfume or after shave, the aroma of freshly filtered coffee or newly baked bread — the list is endless. These are everyday matters which we all encounter and which most of us have little or no difficulty in coping with satisfactorily. But many clients do suffer because they appraise harmless circumstances as being threatening or associate them with some harm or loss. In other words, clients create harmful situations out of harmless ones — and suffer the consequences. Why should this be so? How do they do it?

As we have observed, it is the personal meaning that clients attribute to the events they are appraising which leads to their being experienced as problems. In our NLP counselling sessions we find our clients frequently confirm the dictum of the first-century philosopher Epictetus who said, 'People are disturbed not by things but by the views which they take of them.' Nowhere is this more evident than in those clients who genuinely suffer personal stress as a consequence of appraising harmless circumstances as being threatening and potentially harmful, or indicating impending loss. Sometimes the fear experienced by clients from their personal appraisals of harmless circumstances can be so disabling that they cannot leave home or get up out of bed in the morning. There is a self-evident counselling lesson here for all of us. Whenever we hear or see clients seeming to suffer as the result of harmless circumstances we treat them with respect. We respond genuinely; we listen to what the client is telling us. Most of all we take what they say they are experiencing very seriously.

Conditioned Habits in Clients

●

You may be thinking that many of the examples we have just mentioned could be explained by clients having been conditioned into their habits. In classical conditioning, clients learn to fear harmless situations or have difficulty in retaining mastery over situations which it is completely within their capabilities to handle. Classical conditioning involves reflexes in the autonomic nervous system which fire automatically and are part of our natural 'fight–flight' survival system. It is part of a primitive psychobiological mechanism that allowed our ancestors to take flight or stand and fight to survive, and which we still have today. This fits well with classical conditioning and the problems of clients who come to NLP counselling. Knowing about the original discovery of classical conditioning by the great Russian physiologist Ivan Pavlov helps us put this in perspective.

Pavlov presented the harmless sound of a bell to a dog and at the same time placed some dried meat powder in the dog's mouth. The dog salivated and ate the food. After several such paired presentations the bell alone was presented, but no dried meat powder. The dog still salivated, as it would if the meat powder was there. Pavlov had made a great discovery. He claimed that the dog had learned a conditioned response. The unconditioned stimulus, meat, produced an unconditioned response — salivation. The conditioned stimulus — the bell *in the absence of the unconditioned stimulus* — produced a conditioned salivation in the dog. In essence the dog had learned to salivate at the sound of the bell. Now our interest in this experiment for NLP counselling is with the principle that an apparently irrelevant stimulus can produce a certain response. Extending the principle, we find that harmless or benign situations can produce in clients unpleasant emotional responses such as anxiety and fear. We find that clients in NLP counselling often complain of experiencing phobias, fears and anxiety and that they know they should not feel the way they feel because the situations they find distressing and disabling are apparently harmless. Certainly many clients who come to counselling are suffering from problems they have learned to produce through classical conditioning in otherwise harmless circumstances.

NLP Counselling: Going Beyond the Obvious
●

In our view the NLP counsellor needs to go beyond the apparent classical conditioning of clients and pursue other questions in counselling. The NLP counsellor and client also need to know what the 'harmless' situations are that produce their problems, what the 'harmless' situations mean to the client, and how clients manage to produce problems they experience from apparently neutral circumstances. We believe that, for clients to evoke anxiety phobias, worries, happiness, sadness, elation and other experiences, they must first engage in personal cognitions. It is the personal cognitions of clients which produce the information which they can attribute meaning to in their lives. Clients decide 'This is a dangerous or threatening situation with which I can or cannot cope' and behave accordingly. They imbue their circumstances with their personal meaning. They may do this through choice or in a habitual way. When they do so habitually, this may mean responding to harmless situations as if they were full of harm. In NLP counselling we regard conditioned habits such as these as patterns of meaning and behavioural response. The task for NLP counsellors is to specify the pattern with the client and find ways of changing the meaning it has for them and how it is represented in their personal reality.

This is not always an easy task. Clients may have lost contact with the set things or circumstances or people that they regard as having created their present problems. They may even have distressing and habitual reactions to their memories of the past, fear of the present and uncertainty about the future. On the other hand, we have found that clients can be acutely aware of the appraisals they make and the personal significance internal and external events have for them. It is the clients' personal appraisals that generate the meaning their experience has for them and their relationships. This is the way in which clients make sense of their behaviour and the world in which they live. As NLP counsellors we therefore need to consider the particular personal cognitions of clients and their representations of reality. This is one of the primary tasks in NLP counselling. The NLP counsellor needs to understand the way clients construct their personal–cognitive–behavioural map of reality. NLP counsellors are frequently concerned with a fundamental question: How are these clients making sense of themselves, their problems and their reality?

Chapter 2

THE MAP IS NOT THE TERRITORY

Client Maps and Multiple Realities
●

It is our experience that clients come to NLP counselling with their own cognitive–neurolinguistic maps of reality. It is these maps of reality that make up their model of the world. No two maps are exactly the same, but many of the features on their cognitive–neurolinguistic maps are shared and these form the basis for 'understanding the client' and the client 'understanding the counsellor'. To begin, continue and realize client outcomes, NLP counsellors need to be good map readers. More than this, they need to utilize whatever resources are necessary for clients to reshape, redraw and make changes to what they assume to be their reality and the so-called 'problems' they face. We have referred to clients as experiencing an assumed reality and having so-called problems. We now need to demonstrate what we mean. In NLP counselling, demonstrations are worth more than a million explanations.

Consider a geographical map for a moment. Look in the index of the atlas for a country, for example some faraway place like Brazil. You find the page with a shape on it and green, blue and brown colours and the word 'Brazil' printed on the page. Now have you found Brazil? Do you know what Brazil is like? Is Brazil that little square you found that intersects with the other little square on page 33, the one that corresponds to the name in the index? Ask someone else how you find Brazil. Ask someone who has been to Brazil what it is like. They will not say that Brazil is the map printed on a certain page in different colours, a small square in the middle of the world. For them Brazil may be 'found' by experiencing its culture. They may know what Brazil is like because they stayed with a Brazilian family. They may say Brazil is the last heartbeat of the natural world. But whatever they say about how you find Brazil and what it is like, none of it will be like the geographical map. What they have is their own map of what Brazil is: how it can be found and what it means to them — which illustrates nicely a practical principle in NLP counselling. The map is not the territory.

Client Representations Create Many Realities

●

Clearly, then, the shapes, symbols and colours on maps are only representative of the territory on the map. In NLP counselling it is the same with clients. There are many client maps and many client territories. No one map is better or worse than another, no one map more true or false, more ugly or beautiful. There is a story told about the celebrated artist Pablo Picasso that vividly endorses these points on clients and their personal maps. An admirer of Picasso's had taken some box camera photographs of his wife and taken them along to Picasso for the great man to consider, with a view to painting her. As he handed the photographs to Picasso he immediately started to extol the virtues of his wife. He said how big and beautiful his wife was and gave a personal assurance to Picasso that the photographs were an exact likeness of her. Without hesitation, still holding the photographs in his hand, Picasso turned to the man and said that he thought his wife was very ugly and asked, if they were an exact likeness, why was his wife so small? A clear case of the map not being the territory. Client maps represent their personal territories — their inner life and the thoughts, feelings and meanings they associate with it. They are their reality.

Clients and Counsellors in Confusion
●

Clients, and sometimes counsellors, forget that their personal maps are simply representations of reality. A great confusion can occur between counsellors and clients. It can happen at any stage of the counselling process with NLP. It is to be avoided. Counsellors may accept their own map and territory as being that of the client. At this point a client may be confused into believing the counsellor's map of her problems represents the territory the counsellor should work with to 'help' the client overcome her personal problems.

Take a practical example. A client comes to a counsellor with a problem: she cannot get to sleep at night. The counsellor refers to his own map, picking out the 'clients with sleep problems' file from his mind and inspects this file for causes and solutions. The counsellor starts to pursue the line of therapy that assumes people who have sleep problems are anxious or depressed, or both. The client's map is different from the counsellor's. What is her map of the problem? In this case let us assume that the client is not sleeping well because she has just won a scholarship to study at the Royal College of Music and Drama. The territory is feelings of excitement, visions of creativity, and rehearsing for a part in her sleep, and hearing the praise or disapproval of her tutor. This is a different territory from the counsellor's as well as a different map. Far from finding a solution to the problem, we have the counsellor and the client working from different maps of what the problem is and the territory it covers and the way it is represented in their experience. In our experience such a mismatch does happen in counselling and practical counselling with NLP is no exception. A client who is familiar with their map and the territory it represents will help the counsellor retrace and reroute their counselling efforts with the client.

How many times have we heard clients say, with their mouths and their bodies, "No, you haven't understood me"; "No, that is not quite what I meant"; "You have no idea what I am feeling". "No, I experience it differently, I see a picture of them together in my head and that makes me angry", or "I don't see pictures the way you have been suggesting — with me it's hearing the way they talk behind my back: I actually hear the words in my head and that makes me feel sick." These, and many more examples we could all cite, are all instances of mapping and territory mismatches.

What happens when we get a good match in mapping problems and solutions with the client and the territory that their psychoneurolinguistic map represents? The magical result is rapport. The client feels, hears or sees that they are understood. How do we know? The information and feedback we get from the client changes. Instead of mismatching responses we get matching ones. For example, the client says: "Yes, yes, you understand me; it is such a relief to be understood at last"; "You have a clear idea of what I am going through"; "It seems that you can imagine the torment I am in right now"; "Yes, that's right. I do have these pictures of them in bed together in my head"; "That's right, they say it is OK but I am hearing a disapproving tone in everything they say." The majority of the clients that come to our NLP counselling clinics want one thing. They want to change what they experience.

Reframing: the Redrawing of Personal Maps

●

When clients can redraw their personal maps they can experience the psychological territory they occupy differently. An NLP technique that comes close to this is the practice of *reframing*. The Picasso story is an excellent example of reframing. In NLP counselling, reframing can be used extensively with many clients. Reframing changes the way reality is experienced by them, nudging client perception in a different direction. Sometimes reframing can radically alter the lives of clients.

However as Paul Watzlawick (1978) points out, 'reframing is not an interpretation in the classic psychotherapeutic sense; it "deciphers" nothing and does not uncover the "true" meaning hidden behind allegoric, symbolic or bizarre facades'. Reframing is more about recreating cognitive appraisals and therefore offers clients fresh choices: to change what was regarded as unchangeable. Watzlawick says of reframing: 'It breaks the illusory frame inherent in any world image and thereby reveals that what appeared unchangeable can indeed be changed and that there exist superordinate alternatives.'

Experiencing Reframing

One way of experiencing the fundamentals of reframing is for you to do a simple practical experiment. Look at a map of a place you have never been to before. First of all hold it upside down and try to read it and make sense of it. Do this for a few moments — no longer than a minute. Now quickly turn the map the 'right' way up and spend the same amount of time looking at it. What happened? Maybe now you recognize the place; you could read the writing on the map; you could comprehend the outlines of the land and rivers, the mountains and valleys. Yet it was the same territory represented by the same map. By reorienting or reframing the map you could see and understand something differently, something that had not in any of its representational features changed. What had changed was the way you looked at it. The way you changed your frame of reference gave you a different experience. Change your frame of reference and you change your mind. Change your mind and you change your experience. Reframe your personal map and you change the experience of your territory. This is the essence of reframing. It is a powerful part of NLP counselling.

Clients in NLP counselling usually participate well in reframing their experience provided you have rapport and are working from their representations of reality. You can use reframing to match or change the cognitive representations clients make of their realities. Reframing can also be used to work with changing clients' attitudes, beliefs, thinking, feelings and behaviour. At the sensory representation level, reframing is also a useful technique for counselling clients through visual, auditory, kinaesthetic, and olfactory frames of reference. Below we consider some examples of reframing.

Table 1: Examples of reframing	
Client frame of reference	**Counsellor reframe**
I can't, I am too anxious	It is good that you are able to be sensitive to the way you are feeling
I am so confused ...	Confusion often leads to new learnings
Everything is too complicated	Maybe that tells you now is the time to do something simple
My anger just gets me in trouble	Your anger has brought you here for help
I see things that upset me	You have clearly focused on something that matters to you
People laugh at me because I am a dreamer ...	You know Einstein discovered the theory of relativity in a dream
I suffer so much from a chronic fear of ...	So there is a perceptive part of you that knows when to tell you are at risk
I will fail because I am so nervous ...	It is so important to be anxious enough to concentrate ...
He will never speak to me again ... I was so cruel ...	He has realized the strength of your feelings
I believe I will never make a good parent	Good parents often doubt their abilities. It is a sign of sensitivity

Table 1: Examples of reframing (continued)	
Client frame of reference	**Counsellor reframe**
He has got too stop breaking things and having tantrums	A tantrum is a way of asking for a different solution to his problems
I hear nothing I like — our relationship has turned sour	Your listening ... says there is a sweeter side to life
I can't bear to look at him anymore; he makes my flesh creep ...	Closing your eyes can let you concentrate on your inner voice ... and it can move you to action ...
I have this sick feeling swirling inside me ... I'm so tensed and coiled up ...	It helps to have a signal that tells you it is time to unwind
I feel like a prisoner ...	A prisoner knows the value of freedom ...
I keep wanting to rewrite the past. I feel so guilty ...	Guilt is a way of nudging you towards experiencing a new chapter in your life ...
The trouble is I keep bottling up my real thoughts and feelings	You seem to be able to control yourself so well ...
He disagrees with everything I say and I disagree with everything he says	Yes, true ... there are many different ways of saying things ...

The Significance of Reframing

●

Reframing is not just a device to enable clients to feel better about themselves, think about their concerns differently or change their attitudes and behaviour. The NLP counsellor's sensitive use of reframing can and does do these things, but the main purpose of reframing is to help clients redraw their maps of reality. In therapy and counselling with NLP there are countless opportunities to use reframing. Often the reframing used by the counsellor spontaneously emerges out of the particular problems clients say they are experiencing or facing and seemingly cannot change.

At other times the NLP counsellor will deliberately create a reframe in anticipation of what a client might say. However, this will usually be after their first counselling session with clients or maybe several sessions into therapy. The main point is that the NLP counsellor shows interest in clients, tries to understand and is curious about the way they frame their difficulties and how these can be usefully reframed for individuals, or families in counselling and their relationships. Clearly, reframing involves a conscious change of viewpoint, or seeing a problem from a different perspective, or hearing the meaning of a personal relationship difficulty in a new way. However the method of making the reframe seems to work on unconscious assumptions which, when a reframe is made, trigger a fresh understanding that was not evident before the reframe took place.

James Redfield (1995) draws on the profound wisdom contained in an ancient Peruvian manuscript. In many ways *The Celestine Prophecy* invites us to reframe the whole of our lives by questioning our lives, what they mean, why we live on the planet, and how we can learn through certain insights to evolve by developing energy and love. The whole book can be seen as a reframe for living and growing. There is a particularly instructive passage in this book which nicely illustrates how reframes can be used with someone who has 'bad' dreams.

After being caught by soldiers and thrown into prison, James Redfield shares a cell with a young Peruvian Indian. Redfield has a horrific dream involving searching for a key, storms, deluge and nearly drowning. Clinging to a cliff-face, he notices that it is surrounded by a beautiful beach and flowering forest, with a river below. He sees the key and falls screaming into the river and sinks, at which point he recalls his experience of waking up:

> I sat up quickly in my cot, gasping for air. The young Indian, apparently already awake, walked over to me.
> 'What is wrong? ' he asked.
> I caught my breath and looked around, realizing where I was. I also noticed that the room had a window and that it was already light outside.
> 'Just a bad dream,' I said.
> He smiled at me as though he was pleased at what I said.
> 'Bad dreams have the most important messages,' he commented.
>
> (Redfield, 1995)

NLP Counselling: Learning to Map Read

●

We can see, therefore, how we can usefully think of NLP counselling with clients as like learning to read a map. And there is so much to learn from map reading, is there not? You need to know the structure and layout of the map. You need to find out the personal territory it covers and how that territory is represented by the person. On a geographical map, you can learn from the scale how much land and sea is covered. You can trace the rivers and roads, rail and air routes between many places. Once you have done that and made references to these various places you can plot their positions and relationships to each other. As you go on to do this with every part of the map that interests you, a structure emerges. Once you know the structure of a client map, you have learned a wonderful set of skills. You can then read the client map. You know where you are and so does the client.

Why bother with learning to read client maps? Is it a waste of time and effort, a dissipation of energy? Not at all. The converse is the case. They are an economical use of the counsellor's time, a focused context for effort and a place where energy can be usefully directed. Robert Pirsig (1974) provides us with a profound map-reading metaphor that we urge you to think about in your work with clients in NLP counselling:

> The main skill is to keep from getting lost. Since the roads are only used by local people who know them nobody complains if the junctions aren't posted. And often, they aren't. When they are it's usually a small sign hiding unobtrusively in the weeds and that's all. County road-sign makers seldom tell you twice. If you miss that sign in the weeds that's *your* problem, not theirs.
>
> (Pirsig, 1974)

NLP Counsellors as Cartographers of Clients

●

Counsellors using NLP need to have, and continue to develop, their client map-reading skills. These are the skills of building rapport and noticing how clients map out their realities and how these are represented in their conscious experience. More than this, NLP counsellors have the task of framing difficulties and gathering information in a way that encourages clients to search for and find solutions in the signs hidden amongst the weeds of their problems. The client may be conscious or unconscious of the signs. Signs are information that empowers clients to map out their reality. Through feedback clients make it possible for the counsellor to comprehend their psychoneurolinguistic maps. As for change, NLP counsellors may work with clients to change little signs in the individual maps that make up their experience or redraw their personal landscape altogether.

NLP Counselling: Magic in Action

●

When NLP counsellors do counselling well they produce 'magical' results in clients. It is interesting that NLP counsellors have indeed been referred to as wizards and magicians. When you watch a magician doing a card trick, if you know how it is done, it is no longer magic. The outcome is only magical because you do not know what is happening. There is a 'magic' which is outside our experience and understanding. There are also magical outcomes in counselling but if you take the counsellor skills and the steps apart it really is quite ordinary, more like a recipe for helping people change.

Like the magician, the NLP counsellor has procedures and skills and they are diligently observed and masterfully practised, with due regard for the welfare of the client. The 'magic' of counselling is client change. The therapist Jay Haley, who wrote *Uncommon Therapy*, a book about Ericksonian therapy, said: 'At one time I considered entitling the book, "Sorcery and Common Sense", as this captured the essence of the therapist and their practice of counselling and psychotherapy.'

Sorcerers and Masterful Magicians of NLP

Magicians need to practise their art. NLP counsellors have to do the same. When first using NLP in counselling we are conscious of the particular procedures and skills we bring into play in our counselling sessions with clients. At this stage we are like apprentice sorcerers. We are eager to learn and we have a lot to learn. To begin with, we may also feel slightly self-conscious and awkward when working with clients: mapping out and framing their realities, gathering information, calibrating their experiences, problems and attempted solutions.There is nothing wrong with this, or with making mistakes, because in using NLP in counselling with clients nothing need ever be wasted. There is no failure in NLP counselling. There is only feedback. Clients and counsellors need to know this and know that they know it. As you read through, and use, this book, judge this for yourselves against your own model of counselling. Be curious and ask yourself what has not been wasted in your counselling sessions and how, specifically, feedback contributed to your work with clients or your ability to conduct NLP counselling.

NLP counsellors help clients to notice things. Clients then see the signs under the weeds. They hear the sound of the wind blowing against the signs. They feel the weight of their problems. NLP counsellors can only do all of these things with the help of their clients. Feedback from the client provides the raw data on which NLP counselling makes progress or falters. Let it be said that in NLP counselling the client is instructor to the counsellor. It is the client's model of reality that the counsellor needs to understand. Providing the counsellor is flexible enough, clients can then make choices and changes that alter their experience and alter the direction of their lives. The degree of mastery in NLP counselling is therefore crucial to the outcome of contacts with clients.

The Apprentice and the Master of NLP Counselling

●

Consider two clients working with NLP counsellors. Both the counsellors are involved in the task of mapping out their clients' problem and reality and how they are represented in their thinking and feelings and the way they behave. Study each case closely and decide where you believe the counsellor is working well with the client map and where the counsellor is trying to impose his own understandings and his own map of what the client is thinking and feeling and the changes she needs to make in her behaviour.

Client Mapping: First Counsellor

COUNSELLOR: Jane where would you like to begin?

JANE: I don't really see where I can begin it is so difficult, vague and ... and confusing.

COUNSELLOR: Well, maybe I can help. It involves you and Lawrence and you keep arguing, so you wanted to come here to sort out your life with him ...

JANE: That is true, but I know that already. I think it goes deeper than that. Somewhere we lost each other and just keep rowing all the time ... it's no good.

COUNSELLOR: I think you should bring Lawrie in with you next time for your session and we can work something out together ... What do you think?

JANE: No! No! That is the last thing I would want — I only have to see his face and we scowl at each other and then we are off on another row. If you want a fight in your clinic, then that is what you would get if you brought us both here at the same time ... In any case, I don't get the picture ... You're not reading me right and in any case Lawrence just detests being called 'Lawrie'...

COUNSELLOR: Jane, believe me, I have vast experience of counselling couples with your sorts of problems and I still think it is best for you to bring ... Law ... er ... Lawrence along to our sessions.

Client Mapping: Second Counsellor

COUNSELLOR: What seems to be the concern that has brought you here today, Raymond?

RAYMOND: I am not really sure. I thought at first it might be my girlfriend ... You could give me some advice about how to handle her when we get into arguments ... We argue a lot ... I am a bit unclear right now ...

COUNSELLOR: That's OK ... I would like to check with you how you are seeing the situation ... You say you know you argue a lot with your girlfriend and maybe you are wondering if it is really your girlfriend that needs some advice ... yet that is something you are unclear about ... and me, I am unclear, so we are both unclear about something at this particular moment. Would that be right?

RAYMOND: Mmm. Yes, that's right ... so I wonder what next?

COUNSELLOR: I wonder if for the next few moments maybe you could imagine that you could see a time when your relationship with your girlfriend was different ...

RAYMOND: Oh, that is no problem. Our relationship has always been a stormy one ... Right from the first time we went out I remember we rowed and rowed ...

COUNSELLOR: That's right. You know that you row ... *and* you know that you have rowed right since you met each other ...

RAYMOND: That's true ... very true.

COUNSELLOR: True. I wonder how you know how to do it?

RAYMOND: Do what?

COUNSELLOR: Have a row with your girlfriend ... Suppose she was here right this minute ... You say you would row — how would you do it?

RAYMOND: Oh, I know only too well what would happen. We would say hello and she would start telling me how marvellous my brother Dwain is all over again and I would then get this burning feeling in between my shoulders in my back and start shouting and she would start screaming back at me and I would curse her and tell her I was going to pack it in and go back with Donna, my ... ah ... my ... wife ...

COUNSELLOR: That is very interesting, Raymond ... Let's see if you have learned what is emerging so far ... just put it ... in any way that is beginning to make some sense to you ...

Counselling Analyses

What did you notice specifically about the way each counsellor approached mapping out the client reality? Which one was the apprentice NLP counsellor and which the master? What makes you think that?

Making Mistakes

●

Clearly we all make mistakes in counselling. Those beginning in NLP counselling probably make more mistakes than a seasoned counsellor. Mistakes happen, not only in mapping out client realities, but through the sincere, but misinformed interventions adopted by counsellors in an effort to overcome or better manage client problems. Mistakes can also be made by NLP counsellors who are familiar with the problems the client is trying to resolve. The apprentice NLP counsellor probably makes mistakes in counselling because of his ignorance and enthusiasm to 'help' his clients. The master NLP counsellor can still err but this time through his vast knowledge of NLP and the problems clients face in their lives. Paradoxically, then, ignorance and knowledge of NLP counselling are both sources of mistakes that we can make with clients in counselling. Below we consider these typical mistakes.

Mistake Number One: Playing the Expert

We may assume we understand the client's map of reality when we do not. We call this mistake 'playing the expert'. Have you ever done this? A client comes to you for counselling. They have barely begun to give you an idea of their map of reality when you are telling them you know all about their problem and how to fix it. Maybe you do, maybe you don't. And maybe you have not played the expert — but as you read this you can perhaps think of someone you know who you might say indulges in playing the expert in counselling clients.

What are the drawbacks for clients when we play the expert?
Are there some benefits for clients if we play the expert?
Under what circumstances would an NLP counsellor play the expert?

Mistake Number Two: Being Technically Correct

Mistake number two is one which we have observed in ourselves and others during our early training in NLP counselling and psychotherapy. We want to be technically correct. We keep it in mind that we need to build rapport with clients. We are alert and on the lookout for information. As avid information gatherers, we enthusiastically apply ourselves to getting information from the client. On top of this we have a vast number of NLP techniques we vigorously employ when counselling clients. All technically correct. But there is a huge problem: we are so preoccupied with pursuing the logistics and practising the technology of NLP that we have lost contact with the client. Have you ever wondered why some counsellors just seem to be technically very skilful yet their clients take a very long time to change or may not change during their course of counselling? What is particularly worrying is that they may even get worse.

This is one of the reasons why regular and vigilant supervision is required for counsellors using NLP. It is important that they are able to move through the necessary stages of acquiring technique and competence to a blending of their skills that appear to flow naturally and seamlessly in their counselling sessions with clients. Outstanding therapists like Milton Erickson and Carl Rogers, Virginia Satir and Fritz Perls integrated the techniques of counselling and psychotherapy so well within themselves that they lived their therapy. If we may be permitted a cliché, they *were* their therapy. They were therapeutic magicians.

On the way to becoming a counselling magician, NLP counsellors need to be aware of being technically correct and clear about the NLP techniques they use in counselling clients. However we should always keep our essential purpose clearly in mind: to explore, understand and act within the client's map of reality. As Alfred Adler has succinctly observed, the personal concerns and solutions for people and their problems lie within their 'schema of apperception' and not that of the therapist. In NLP counselling, when we stray too far from the client's map of reality, we lose our way.

Mistake Number Three: Believing the Map is the Territory

Probably one of the most typical mistakes we can make as NLP counsellors is to believe the map is the territory it represents. Aldous Huxley (1977) asks us to notice that we can become bedevilled by a reduced sense of awareness, so much so that we are inclined to believe in a sense of reality where we are too apt to take our concepts as data, and our words for actual things. Let us consider an example. A woman comes to you for counselling. You build rapport and, while giving information in your first counselling session, she tells you her husband has left her and is never coming back. Now some NLP counsellors would assume that the woman would be upset and feel anxious that her husband should return to his home and his previous life. Other NLP counsellors would just not know the woman's feelings or her thoughts about her experience that she had described.

Now let us say that the woman says she was glad he had left and that she was fed up with him beating her every time he got drunk — and he got drunk every Friday night. On Friday nights she knew she would end up getting punched and kicked by him. This little vignette with the client nicely reveals how we can genuinely end up mistaking the map for the territory it represents. What does this mistake tell us? First, what clients tell us can often mean different things to them from the meaning inferred by the counsellor. Second, the language of the client is part of the way they map out their experience and communicate to counsellors. Third, the experiences clients have or may not have in mapping out their problems and concerns belong to and are those of the client. Fourth, mistaking the map for the territory can be seductive; some NLP counselling may get stuck, repeating this error with clients.

What else does mistaking the map for the territory tell you about your counselling of clients?
Write down what comes to mind.
Share and compare your thoughts with colleagues.

The Importance of Supervision
●

You may find that you want to work through the mistakes in NLP counselling with your supervisor at your next personal supervision sessions. Although this is not a book about supervision, we should like to emphasize the need for appropriate, regular supervision in NLP counselling. Counsellors should also have the opportunity of continuous professional development and training if they are to correct their mistakes and become, and continue to be, expert in their work with clients.

Making the Most of Our Mistakes: Learning to Correct Ourselves

●

Making mistakes in NLP counselling is not failure. Mistakes are a valuable source of feedback for counsellors and clients. Mistakes in counselling with NLP provide us with wonderful opportunities for new learning. New learning offers counsellors the choice of doing something different with clients.

For clients new learning brings about alternative ways they can be thinking and feeling about their problems and the behaviours they engage in to run their lives. In NLP counselling, mistakes are necessary for change. Mistakes form the basis for changing client maps and the realities clients experience. In NLP we need to know our mistakes, know that we know our mistakes, and learn from our mistakes so we can avoid repeating them again and again.

In NLP language, counsellors create conditions where clients can identify their patterns that prevent them achieving their outcomes. When they have done this, new personal patterns can be introduced and integrated into client maps to realize the outcomes they choose for themselves and others.

Let There Be Light

●

As we were writing this we were reminded of the story of Thomas Edison and the light bulb. Edison continued with his experiments to invent the light bulb in the face of being labelled a failure. He made literally thousands of mistakes. One journalist is supposed to have asked him why he pursued his fruitless experiments and passionately continued with them after 'failing' so many times. Edison is said to have patiently replied, "My dear young man, there is something you don't understand. I haven't failed. I have successfully discovered 5000 ways that won't work!" Eventually Edison found the blueprint that led to the mapping out of experiments that were eventually successful. The electric light bulb shone and has lit up the world ever since.

Mapping client realities may mean we make as many as 5000 mistakes in counselling clients. But as NLP counsellors we can learn about and from these mistakes. At times discovering and working with client maps of reality will seem to lead us nowhere. But we can be like Thomas Edison. We can be curious about our mistakes. We can appreciate learning from our mistakes in NLP counselling as many times as we have to, until we reach the client on her own ground, in her own place and in her own territory.

Chapter 3

REPRESENTING REALITY: THE FOUNDATIONS OF EXPERIENCE

Perception and Experience in NLP Counselling
●

Clients do not usually come to counselling and start talking to you about their personal maps. What they do instead is talk about their experiences: what they experienced in the past, what they are experiencing now and what they may experience in the future. These are experiences they may mean to continue to have or they may be experiences they want less of. They may also be experiences they never want to have or repeat again. Much of the time, as counsellors, we find that clients in counselling say they have problems and want to be rid of the experiences they are undergoing or have undergone for days, months or even years. In NLP counselling we hear clients saying they are suffering from anxiety, depression, stress and anger. Clients tell us that they are in 'bad' relationships and want to get out of them. They may also claim that they are in conflict with their children, their friends, colleagues at work, relatives and spouses. And some clients say they are in pain and traumatized from the crises they have had to face in their lives or are victims of abuse and addiction.

Clients tell us these are the problems they face and fear and fail at overcoming. Clearly not every problem people face can be overcome through counselling, but nothing can be overcome unless it is faced. Counselling offers clients the opportunity to overcome their personal problems. These and many other personal difficulties and the way clients describe them to counsellors are the typical content of counselling sessions, whatever the approach adopted by counsellors. However, there are essential differences in the way NLP counselling is conducted and in the assumptions underlying the counselling process. First, although clients describe their problems in a similar way, the problems they face are not exactly the same. Second, the way clients experience their problems varies considerably, the perception of each person being unique. Third, the solutions to problems described by clients are individual to each client. Fourth, and fundamental for NLP counsellors, interventions that lead to solutions chosen by clients are also individual to the client in counselling. There are no standard client problems and no standard client solutions. As a further consequence of this, we can conclude there are no standard counsellor interventions when we are using NLP counselling.

Separate Realities
●

Many counsellors will appreciate the old dictum, 'Some clients are like all clients some of the time, and all clients are like some clients some of the time, but no client is like any other client all of the time. Each client is unique.' This may be confirmed in your everyday experience with people and as practising counsellors and therapists. In our NLP counselling clinics we have frequently noticed how clients have their own personal maps, their own reality. Those counsellors working within an NLP frame of reference in counselling therefore need to be able to answer three fundamental questions:

1 How are the many and varied personal maps that clients bring to counselling created?
2 How can we tell which map a client bases their present experience of reality upon?
3 What is the difference that can be made to change their experience of reality?

Carlos Castaneda (1985), in speaking of his many learnings from his mentor Don Juan, says:

> He was very careful to establish that the world was whatever we perceive, in any manner we may choose to perceive. Don Juan maintained that "perceiving the world" entails a process of apprehending whatever presents itself to us. This particular perceiving is done with our senses and with our will.'
> (Castaneda, 1985)

The Senses: Filters of Personal Perception

Reality in NLP counselling is perceived reality. Problems seem real enough to clients who believe they have problems and can find no satisfactory solution to them. The NLP counsellor does not ignore or deny that clients experience real pain and may be confused and desperate to find a better way of living their lives, but it is the way clients construct their reality and problems and how pain, turmoil, confusion, stress and trauma are represented and expressed by clients that are of critical interest in counselling with NLP.

As we discover how a client's personal map of reality is constructed, we are in a better position to understand her and help her to heal herself, or change and take more direct action. We have found in our own work that clients' perceptions of themselves frequently arise from their five senses, the filters through which their sense of reality and their present state are experienced and expressed. A few examples help to demonstrate the importance of the senses in forming the foundation of self-perception.

Client A

Client A comes to you for counselling and says, "I am very depressed and anxious. My problem is I see my future as very bleak and a black cloud is hanging over me right now."

Client B

Client B comes to counselling and says, "I am very depressed and anxious. My problem is I hear this little voice inside my head

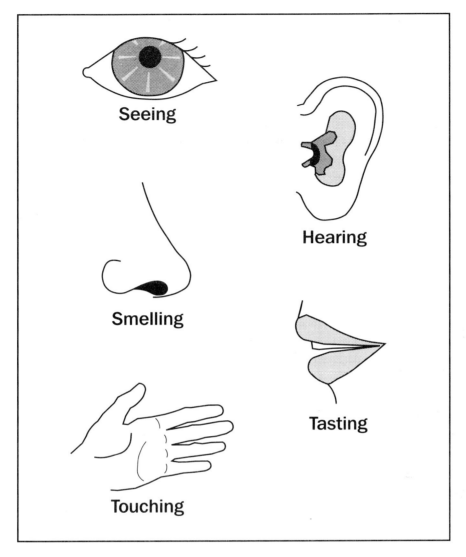

Figure 2 *NLP and the five senses*

telling me I am no good and it shouts at me to give up trying to solve my problems."

Client C

Client C says, "I am very depressed and anxious. My problem is I feel it right here in my body [*points to throat and chest*]. My body, it's like a ton weight and it's dragging me down. It's like crying inside — it hurts."

Client D

Client D says, "I am very depressed and anxious. My problem is the stench of the bodies from the flames in the air crash keeps coming back to me and whenever this happens I get this, well, depressed and anxious. I can't bear being near anybody cooking meat or anything like that — it just makes me worse."

These examples from clients provide useful information for NLP counsellors. First, they show us that clients communicate in counselling with sense-based representations. Second, clients may represent their experience through the visual, auditory, kinaesthetic or olfactory senses. A third observation is that clients often have a preferred way of representing their experiences through their sensory processes. Finally, the way in which the senses are represented for each client is unique to them. However a similarity is that the senses are interrelated in a complex set of communications, and the way information is imparted and choices are made by clients forms part of a more comprehensive sensory representational system. In the clinic it is more often the case that clients represent their experience by using a combination of the senses available to them.

For example, a client might say: "I get angry. Just the sight of him makes my blood rush to my head and I get this tight feeling here in my chest. When I get this I am mad. It's a kind of smouldering ... you could almost choke on the smoke coming out of me. Each time I think about it I hear myself saying, "Oh no, we are about to have a blow-out again — I know a row is coming on." How many senses were used to represent reality by this client?

Thinking and Sensory
Representational Systems
●

NLP counselling also makes the assumption that we think in systems. These may be logical and linear systems; they may be more diverse systems of association; they may be systems of thinking that are represented idiosyncratically by each individual;

but they all share the sensory framework of visual, auditory, kinaesthetic and olfactory systems in the way they represent their reality and their experience.

In their breakthrough book, *The Structure of Magic II*, Grinder and Bandler refer to sensory perceptual systems as the basic elements through which we form our behaviour. We think in sensory perceptual terms, and sensory systems provide the feedback and filtered information upon which we think and act. Sensory representational systems are the building-blocks of counsellor and client behaviour. Sight, hearing, body sensations, smell and taste provide us with the gateways to knowledge about ourselves and others. In NLP counselling, the knowledge that can be brought to counselling sessions is usually derived from these sensory representational systems and is known symbolically as a 4-tuple:

$$<V\ (e,\ i),\ A\ (e,\ i),\ K\ (e,\ i),\ O\ (e,\ i)>$$

The 4-tuple is a useful formula that is easy to understand and captures the central part sensory representational systems play in NLP counselling and working with the clients' maps and models of their present reality. In NLP counselling the 4-tuple is often simply referred to by its sensory representational acronym, VAKO.

Let us break the 4-tuple down bit by bit. The symbols at the extreme left and right signify that at any time there may be a lesser or greater amount of activity in any one of the sensory representational systems within them. The capital letters are simply abbreviations showing the different classes of sensory representational systems:

V = Visual
A = Auditory
K = Kinaesthetic
O = Olfactory/Gustatory

The *e, i,* notation in each set of parentheses within the 4-tuple indicates that representations may come from sources that are *external* or *internal* to clients or counsellors.

	Vi	**Ai**	**Ki**	**Oi**
Ve	VeVi	VeAi	VeKi	VeOi
Ae	AeVi	AeAi	AeKi	AeOi
Ke	KeVi	KeAi	KeKi	KeOi
Oe	OeVi	OeAi	OeKi	OeOi

Figure 3 *Internal and external VAKO matrix*

External and Internal Sources of Client Reality

By external we mean those representations that clients make when they are experiencing through their senses something that is coming from outside themselves. Internal NLP representations in the 4-tuple are those which clients are generating within themselves without any necessary reference to the external world. Clients who are representing their reality with an internal 4-tuple remember, imagine or create in their minds pictures, sounds, feelings, tastes and smells from the past or present, or create them for the future. The 4-tuple is of immense importance in working with clients in NLP counselling.

There can be many combinations of 4-tuple — internally or externally generated, or both. They can all be useful to the NLP counsellor who is mapping out the perceptual basis of client experience and the changes that clients may want to make in the way they experience their reality. Look at the VAKO matrix (Figure 3) and think for a moment about the range of ways in which it can be useful in counselling clients.

Sometimes clients will represent their experience to themselves through one sensory representational system. For example, a client may say they recall an accident they had as a series of disjointed pictures. They may not have feelings associated with the accident. They may not hear the voices of the people who helped at the scene of their accident. They experience in individual counselling a single representation of the event they are recalling. Other instances of this can occur in counselling. A client who has been the victim of a shooting may not be able to recall the event but will engage in prolonged bouts of crying whenever people ask how she is coping with her trauma. In a representation of their experience in individual counselling, clients think of the event and they get pictures; a person mentions a shooting and they burst into tears.

However people usually tend to represent their experiences through multiple use of their sensory representational systems. When they do so their representations of their experience often overlap and appear to meld together at times. A client will perhaps start by explaining their problem to the counsellor in individual terms and then quickly relate this to angry or anxious feelings they have, but at the same time they do not know what to say to themselves that will help them through a particular problem they experience as stressful or traumatic. This overlapping in NLP counselling is called synaesthesia. The organization and sequence of synaesthesias are individual to each client; in NLP counselling they are known as strategies. One of the essential tasks for NLP counsellors is to provide a climate of counselling where clients can gain access to information which informs them of the strategies they are using. These strategies reveal how clients produce their pain and their pleasure, their hopes and their fears, their plights and their problems.

Sensory Representational Strategies

●

Clients may consciously or unconsciously engage in producing sensory representational strategies that are personal to them. These strategies tell them when they have a problem, what sort of problem it is and when they have overcome or are better at managing their personal problems. For counsellors the ways clients represent their problems sensorily are clear signposts as to the way rapport can be built, appropriate information located and the means by which clients can resolve the difficulties they experience. A glance back at Figure 3 will help you to consider just some of the many different ways your clients can represent their problems when they come to counselling.

The VeVi Representation

Clients producing a reality based on *VeVi* representations present the counsellor with a visually external representation that triggers a synaesthesia with an internal visual representation of their experience. For example, a client who says that, when she sees a romantic film on television, she also sees an image inside her head of the broken romance she has been trying to cope with, is demonstrating a *VeVi* synaesthesia.

The VeAi Representation

A *VeAi* representation occurs when a client produces an external visual representation followed by an auditory internal one. This form of synaesthesia is quite common. For instance, one client who attended our clinic to find out how to control his anger described his problem as being generated by seeing his girlfriend talking to other men and then getting a voice inside his head which told him that she was 'just like your mother — making a fool of you' and that he should 'throw her out of the house'. He said he could hear his mother's voice advising him in the background that women who talked with other men were not to be trusted.

The VeKi Representation

A synaesthesia we frequently find with clients is the *VeKi* representation. This is where the client initially represents their experience in an externally visual way and overlaps into an internally generated kinaesthetic modality. A client once recalled that she was getting along much better in her relationship with her husband until she saw his former mistress in the street. At the sight of 'the other woman' all the old feelings of hurt, anger and lack of confidence came flooding back. She was now requesting further NLP counselling as she wanted help in changing the way she experienced chance meetings with her husband's former mistress.

The VeOi Representation

A man who had been making progress in overcoming a recent divorce had setbacks whenever he saw photographs of his wife. Now this was a problem because his children loved showing him photos of their mother and getting out the 'family album' at the weekends. Whenever the man saw the photographs he could immediately smell the perfume his ex-wife used. This generated longings and sadness at the memories he experienced. He wanted help to overcome his bouts of sadness 'brought on' by the photographs and perfume. Interestingly, his external visual representation overlapping with an internal olfactory representation continued to be a problem for him until he met someone else who used the same perfume.

The AeVi Representation

Our work also involves working with company employees. Often they come to counselling because of changes that are taking place in their organization: they say they cannot cope; they have serious personal stress problems; they miss deadlines; they seem overworked, fatigued and cannot concentrate; they worry; they do not sleep well. When we have traced the sensory representations at the root of their worries we have on occasions found a synaesthesia based on an auditory external representation that overlaps with a visual internal one. For instance, someone hears that all the jobs in his section of the factory are to disappear and be replaced by fully computerized systems of production. He then goes around, sometimes for weeks and months, seeing pictures inside his head of losing his job and not finding another. For many employees this can lead to considerable stress, which they take home with them. As a result family life suffers and there are unwanted tensions and rows at home. Sometimes we can help these clients very quickly by giving them a simple task: find out whether what you hear is true or just idle gossip.

The AeAi Representation

This sensory representation has a synaesthesia that can be usefully understood by referring to it as the external–internal dialogue. One rueful client called it 'the infernal dialogue'. It happens like this. A client is told by his wife that she needs to get away for a rest, mainly from the strain of bringing up their two young children, aged two and four. He then extends this into his own internal dialogue and what he hears inside his mind is his wife saying over and over again that she is fed up with him and probably wants a divorce. He adds to this that he is no good as a husband and continues this inner dialogue until he can bear it no longer and gets drunk. His internal talk is his problem — not his marriage.

The AeKi Representation

In NLP counselling the synaesthesia of an external sensory auditory representation being converted to an internal kinaesthetic one is not unusual. Let us consider an excerpt from a real case. A client came to our counselling and psychotherapy clinic who said she was suffering from a phobia. She said she had 'stage fright' and froze when giving any public speech or seminar or even in an informal gathering of friends where she was expected to talk. She found her tongue froze in her mouth — it just would not move. It turned out quite clearly how her map of reality produced her frozen state. When she was a little girl she had heard from her grandmother, of whom she was terrified, that little girls have their tongues tied in a big knot when they talk too much.

The AeOi Representation

The synaesthesia obtained from an external auditory sensory representation moving into an olfactory one can be easily experienced by reference to daily life. When someone asks what you had for dinner last night, you might, as you recall it, smell the food you are describing. The synaesthesia can be intensified if you are hungry and someone asks you about the dinner you are going to cook tonight. One client we worked with had a very unpleasant *AeOi* synaesthesia. She was in the process of overcoming the death of her beloved brother. However, whenever anyone spoke his name and asked how she was managing with the changes taking place in her life, she could smell his body odour. To begin with this upset her, but as she made progress in counselling she began to want to bring back the sweet smell of his body as a way of remembering him fondly and the times they spent together.

The KeVi Representation

Some clients who come for counselling do not readily visualize or have an internal dialogue right away, so they cannot get immediate access to the way they 'see' their problems. Others cannot hear themselves being more assertive and talking themselves towards a positive self-image. It is not that they cannot do it — they just have a preferred way of representing their difficulties sensorily that is primarily kinaesthetic, based on feeling, which can often then be followed by getting a picture in their heads. The counsellor needs to be vigilant as regards the *KeVi* synaesthesia. It is more effective than simply asking clients to make a picture in their minds in which they are more assertive and refuse an invitation to drink alcohol.

We recall the single mother of a 14-year-old boy who participated in counselling. She indicated that she was using an external kinaesthetic representation overlapping a visual internal one — all within a few moments of entering the counselling clinic. She said how nice and warm the room felt and how she could see herself and her mother sitting next to the Christmas tree in their home before the family broke up. The counsellor was curious about this and found it to be very significant as counselling progressed. At one point the client described her relationship with her son as cold and she started to shake and said that when they rowed he always gave her an ice-cold stare. She wanted to improve their relationship. At this point the counsellor asked her what she would want to feel as she was creating a warmer feeling with her son. She then got some more internal visual pictures that took her back to her mother again and that gave her more good feelings.

There were other interventions but the counsellor and the client contrived a small but significant change to the draughty flat she lived in with her son. She agreed to keep the temperature at a near constant 20 degrees Celsius throughout the flat. This immediately put her in a better mood and she had far fewer rows with her son.

Now look at the rest of the matrix and provide some of your own examples for the remaining synaesthesias. You may find it helpful to refer to your own clients and ask yourself which aspects of the 4-tuple they use to represent their experiences in counselling sessions. What you find out could be valuable to your clients, providing feedback to them about their use of sensory representational systems and synaesthesias.

Client Synaesthesias

●

We have found the internal and external VAKO matrix a very useful way of mapping out with clients the synaesthesias they use in NLP counselling. Sometimes clients will repeatedly have the same synaesthesias for a specific problem they are describing. For instance, one client could not bear men touching her. When they did, she immediately got an internal visual representation of her father sexually abusing her as a young child. When this happened, further synaesthesias took place. She then had an internal kinaesthetic representation of nausea and wanted to be sick.

There are a number of points we would like to make here. First, clients can have one particular synaesthesia, often associated with a particular problem. Second, we find that clients can also move rapidly from one sensory representation system to another when describing their problems. There are therefore single and multiple synaesthesias. The single synaesthesia is the snapshot, the multiple synaesthesia the movie.

Counselling with NLP allows us to analyse the personal strategies that clients are using to create their realities. The way clients deploy their sensory representational systems and the synaesthesias they produce are an essential part of understanding clients and the world within which they live. Much more than this, however, they provide the counsellor with a basis for NLP processes from which many counselling interventions can arise and client change can take place.

Indicators of and Access to
Sensory Representational Systems
●

How do we know which sensory representational system a client is using at any one time? This is a perfectly reasonable question and one that needs answering. One way is to listen very closely to what the client says and match the language of sensory representation with what the client is doing. The case examples and the 4-tuple matrix gave us plenty of clues about the particular sensory representational systems the client was using, but how does the NLP counsellor know or, at least, have a very good idea about the way that a specific client gains access to a particular sensory representational system? What are the indicators? There are two questions in one here. They are both of fundamental importance to the NLP counsellor. First, we need to know how a client accesses a particular sensory representational system. Second, we need to know how that information is given meaning. We call the first of these *the lead system* and the second *the primary representation system*.

The lead system is the sensory window through which information is brought to the attention of the individual. The primary representational system is the means by which meaning is given to the information the individual is attending to and the preferred way of making decisions. An example should help us appreciate the place of the lead system and the part it plays in bringing information to the primary representational system. Celia tells us she is experiencing too much pressure at work and this is giving her a lot of stress. In the course of finding out more about Celia and the way she is representing her problem we find out that she has a marked preference for receiving information in auditory form but prefers making her decisions on visual information. In other words, her lead system is auditory but her primary representational system is visual. The NLP counsellor notes that stress is not the real problem for Celia, but it provides us with the context in which the real problem occurs. Here is the problem.

Celia receives information in visual form. She receives lots of written memos and reports and is expected to redraft them and extract their salient points to share with colleagues, write them up in computer files, distribute them and display them on shared computer terminals. Now what we find is that she does much better and experiences less stress when the memos and reports are sent to her on audiotape, because she can then more easily use her lead system, which allows her unblocked and immediate access to her primary representational system, which is visual. In other words, she works better and more 'naturally' when 'she can hear what needs to be done and this allows her to see the way ahead'.

Identifying the Lead Systems and Primary Representational Systems of Clients

A central task for NLP counsellors is to be able to identify the lead systems and representational systems used by clients. In our approach using the person-centred cognitive behavioural model we discussed earlier, we would usually refer to this as the thinking of clients. However, as our case examples show, it can be very useful for clients and counsellors to break down thinking into the different sensory modalities.

Richard Bandler and John Grinder noticed that, when clients process information, they move their eyes in systematic directions, depending on the kinds of personal information they are processing. These systematic eye movements involve individuals searching for information and representing it in their 'thinking' patterns (see Figure 4). In NLP counselling these eye movements are called 'eye accessing cues'. Let us consider some examples.

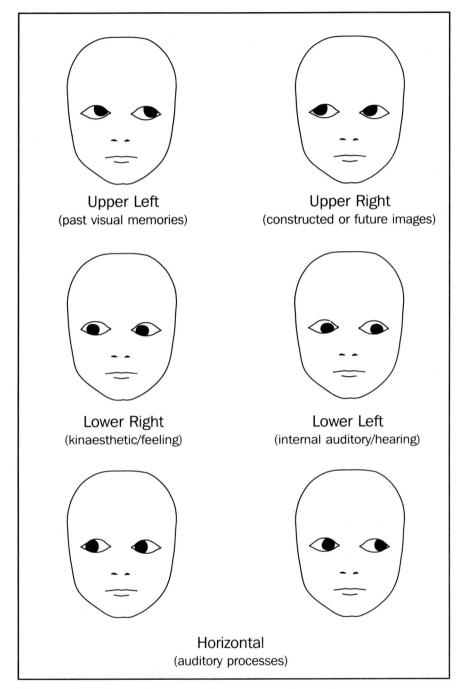

Figure 4 *Accessing sensory systems through eye movement patterns*

VISUALLY REMEMBERED

Clients who remember events visually tend to look up to the left-hand corner when they are retrieving information about the past. A client says to you that her mother had the kindest eyes and you ask "What was the colour of her eyes?" If the client is remembering visually she will typically flick her eyes up and left to get the picture you have asked for before she will answer.

VISUALLY CONSTRUCTED

When constructing visually clients are creating images they have never seen before or seeing things differently in the present from the way they have seen them in the past. Clients may also see themselves in the future being different from the way they are in the present or have been in the past. A client reports to you that she could never imagine herself being confident, although she would like to be. You could then ask her what it would be like to visualize herself as an artist and paint a picture of a very confident and important person from history or the future. You ask her if she can start with the costume and setting and any people, and to see what this confident person is doing. At the very end, you ask your client if she can start colouring the face and as the face becomes clearer she sees it is her face she is looking at.

In this case we would expect the client's eyes to move up and to the right.

AUDITORY REMEMBERING

When clients are using eye movements that flick over to the left, they are engaged in auditory remembering. A client tells you that her boss is always shouting at her and saying horrible things. You discover that this makes the client feel angry and she starts shouting back which leads to lots of arguments at work. During the telling of her story you notice that the client's eyes are frequently flicking over to the left. As an NLP counsellor you take this as a client cue for what to do next. So you ask the client to spend a few more moments getting to know the sound of her boss's voice a little bit more. You ask the client to listen to the voice and describe her experience the last time she heard her boss being angry. If the client is in the auditory remembering mode her eye movements will continue to flick left and back again as she describes her memory of the last time her boss was angry with her.

AUDITORY CONSTRUCTING

Clients who are using the auditory constructing mode are creating new sounds, words, and phrases and communications they have never experienced in the past. They are not retrieving intact memories. They are constructing new combinations in their auditory experiences: they make it up as they go along.

One counsellor provided counselling to a client who had spent many years bravely fighting lymphatic cancer. He was in great pain. He wanted to know how long he had left to live. He was told by his oncology consultant that he had two or three months of life left, at best. In his next counselling session he was asked what it was like for him to recall the experience of being informed that he only had a few months to live. His tired eyes moved right, paused and then, as they flicked back to their central position, he said it was something he could only describe as the consultant's words being like a banshee out of hell calling him to death. An NLP counselling question to create and gain access to auditory constructing with this client could be "What is her voice like when you hear it backwards, as a melody?"

AUDITORY PROCESSES

Clients who are using the auditory modality usually 'talk to themselves' inside their heads. The eye movements for most people in this case are downwards and to the left. A client once came to counselling saying he was suffering from conflict. On the surface he was faced with telling his wife he had lost his job and had been unemployed for the past two months, or carrying on pretending to go to work each morning and coming back each night as he had done for the past ten years. As he described his problem, the NLP counsellor noticed that the client's eyes flicked up left (as with visually remembered) and then quickly down to the left, oscillating in the left corner.

When asked, "How are you seeing things or hearing them as

you are thinking about this problem?" the client said, "I first saw my wife looking angry with me and now I'm having this debate inside my head — whether to tell her or not." He was visually remembering his wife and then using the auditory modality to run through the arguments for and against telling her. Questions with clients who are using this modality involve asking them to amplify what they are hearing and which voice sounds more reassuring, which one quieter and which louder, and how would they need to hear what they are saying to themselves to resolve the conflict they face.

KINAESTHETIC

Usually people who are retrieving information about themselves in the kinaesthetic mode move their eyes down and to the right. Clients reporting feeling depressed often use this visual kinaesthetic process. We have noticed that many of our clients drop their head slightly when they make this eye movement. A helpful way to remember the position for the kinaesthetic mode is to recognize it as the 'down right sad position'.

Kinaesthetics are gaining access to information about their emotions, sense of touch and feelings about, and from, muscle movements in their bodies. Questions that NLP counsellors typically use with these clients are "What does it feel like to have this loss weighing on you right now?" or "What feelings do you have as you think about the problem now/as you think back?"

One client who recently came for counselling spent a large part of her session apparently staring at a spot on the floor just to the right of her chair. The counsellor at first got nowhere with the client until he noticed the 'down right sad position' and started to talk to the spot on the floor.

Clients do not adopt the kinaesthetic mode just for negative emotions — they also do it for positive emotions.

EYE MOVEMENTS IN GENERAL

You can see from Figure 4 and our examples how most people move their eyes when retrieving visual, auditory and kinaesthetic information. You may find a small number of clients use a reversal or mirror image of the movements shown in the eye accessing chart. Clearly, eye accessing information is of immense importance for the counsellor using NLP in their counselling sessions with clients. First of all eye movements provide essential feedback to counsellors about the way the client is retrieving information about herself and her problems. Second, eye movements are significant indicators of the type of information being retrieved and used by clients. Third, tracking systematic eye movement is useful as it helps the counsellor to formulate therapeutic interventions with clients.

Additional Cues for the NLP Counsellor

You should also look and listen for additional cues that indicate how clients are representing their problems and retrieving relevant personal information. As well as the five senses and eye movement, many clients have typical breathing patterns, voice tonalities and head positions that seem to go along with their eye accessing and sensory representations of reality.

BREATHING PATTERNS

For instance, we have found that people utilizing their visual processes tend to breathe higher in the chest and neck areas when they are in counselling. They also tend to take shorter and shallower breaths than 'kinos' do.

Clients making kinaesthetic representations are often accompanied by breathing that comes from lower in their chest and diaphragm. Kinos seem to breathe slower, deeper and each breath seems to last longer.

VOICE TONALITIES

The voice tonalities of clients gaining access to their visual processes also tend to be higher in pitch and slightly faster in tempo than those of kinaesthetics, who speak from deeper down in their diaphragm. The voice seems to come from the chest and is slower, richer and rounder than that of the client who is expressing herself through visual retrieval and representations of reality. It does not come out as clear as this with every client. Also some clients switch their tonalities, breathing and speech patterns as they retrieve different sorts of information and contexts in which they communicate their problems and experience to the counsellor.

HEAD MOVEMENTS

Next time you are counselling clients, notice their head movements. Counselling has sometimes been colloquially described as a head-to-head encounter, but we have come to believe this is much more literally so than we previously thought. We have observed that each client has a range of head positions and movements that seem to go along with their sensory representations of reality and the way they use eye accessing and processing of personal information.

Clients who are retrieving information through their auditory channel may cock their head to the right or left, similar to the way some people tilt their heads when listening to someone on the telephone. For this reason we call it the telephone posture and when the head is moving from side to side we call these telephone posture movements. The first is the snapshot of the auditory mode, the second the movie version of the auditory mode in which clients are representing their realities through personal information.

Many clients move their heads upwards when remembering or constructing visual experiences and others hold their heads quite steady and central when they are concentrating or working with emotionally significant feelings through their kinaesthetic sensory representations of reality. We have found clients adopt many head positions during counselling when they are engaged in the processes of change. These are associated and co-ordinated with client eye movements and their sensory representations of their reality which they bring to counselling.

We have found ten main head positions (see Figure 5) that are of interest and used in counselling clients: central, upward, downward, right lateral, left lateral, right inclined, left inclined, moving up and down, degree of turn and side to side.

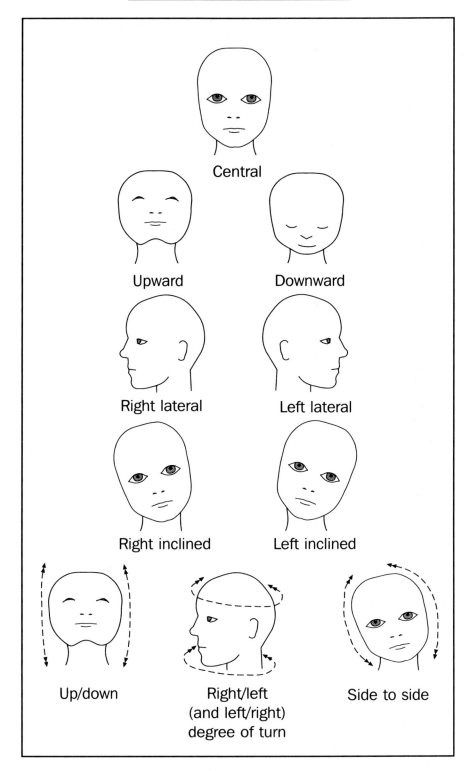

Figure 5 *Main head positions*

Getting Ahead in NLP Counselling:
Learning from the Client

●

Techniques of paying attention to and learning from client head positions are in their infancy in counselling, but we believe they hold out great promise for helping us to understand our clients. We have also discovered that client head movements help us to help them explore their problems. More than this, we would say that knowledge of the significance of head movements can be utilized by NLP counsellors to create alternative realities and personal choices for and with clients in their efforts to accomplish the personal outcomes they wish to experience in their lives.

How do clients represent their problems through their head positions and head movements during counselling sessions? We recall one client who came to our counselling clinic. Each time he said, "Now let me think ..." his head shot up and back about 30 degrees. After a few moments it moved slightly to one side. This was *his* thinking position. He thought in pictures and when he got pictures he could put words to them.

You can see one of the most famous examples of head position in Rodin's sculpture 'The Thinker' (Figure 6). Notice the head position. It is downward. Is it downward and inclined to one side or is it downward and central? What happens to *your* head position when you think? A female client used to say she would have to think the problem through by getting a feeling for the way out of her difficulty. As she was saying this her eyes would drop down to the right. At the same time she would move her head to a right inclined and up and down position.

Each client has their own repertoire of head positions and movements. No two are exactly the same. The important point for the NLP counsellor is to be alert to the changes in clients and the way they represent their realities and bring their 'problems' to counselling sessions. They all form part of that dynamic whole we call the client map of reality. Understanding clients' cognitive maps, their sensory representations of experience and the way sensory information is retrieved through eye and head movements is potentially useful to NLP counsellors and clients. In our view all of these aspects of NLP play an important part in and

Figure 6 *'The Thinker'*

significantly add to the more general processes of client counselling and psychotherapy. They help us to learn from the client and to take appropriate action. Most important of all, they help facilitate the talking part of counselling and psychotherapy — 'The talking cure'.

Chapter 4

NLP COUNSELLING AND THE TALKING CURE

Language, Meaning and Experience

●

Counselling and psychotherapy are often referred to as 'the talking cure'. Some might even say that language is what makes or breaks counsellors' capacity to help clients to help themselves. When we are working with clients we find that using language is like being alongside someone with whom you are travelling on a journey through a foreign land. You take a few steps and before long you need to start orienting yourself. You begin by making some attempts at being understood where you are and the local people try to make themselves understood back to you. Soon you find you are making gestures, noises and intonations, with some words and phrases, and at some point you meet and agree you understand each other. On this basis, and sharing a similar predicament, you proceed. You may be using similar words, but do they mean the same things, and do the same things have different words?

Even in the early stages of counselling clients with NLP you can begin to appreciate that not everyone uses the same words for the same thing or has the same feelings or experiences concerning the same words. Sometimes we find that clients will use only one word or very few expressions to describe many experiences, while others use many words or expressions to describe a single experience they are trying to communicate.

Case Example: A Client of Few Words

KEN: I am blasted.

COUNSELLOR: Mmm, blasted ...

KEN: Yeh, I get blasted a lot.

COUNSELLOR: Everywhere?

KEN: Yeh [*client lets out a short laugh and throws head back and smiles*].

COUNSELLOR: So let me see if I understand. You are blasted. You, now, Ken, you are blasted now and you are blasted all the time and in all places, is that right?

KEN: Dead right.

COUNSELLOR: That blasted experience, you must know that pretty well, and I don't, so I wonder, Ken ... what is that like?

KEN: Well, just blasted ... you know.

COUNSELLOR: Uh ... No, I don't ... but you do ... mmm?

KEN: Yeh ... blasted ... I don't take no shit from anyone.

COUNSELLOR: And that makes you ...

KEN: Makes me feel good, man ... blasted is a good feeling right here [*Ken points to his heart*] Right?

COUNSELLOR: Yeh, right ... so now you know, maybe you could draw that feeling of being blasted right here, here on this paper.

KEN: [*As Ken begins to draw something happens: he speaks more and uses different words*]: This is a picture of me and my sister the last time I saw her alive ... I made a promise to my mother that I would always be happy for her ... each time I didn't feel right, I would get blasted and I would be happy and keep the good feeling for her [*much of the time as Ken is adding more detail to the drawing he says something new*].

COUNSELLOR: A promise ... So being blasted seems so very important, I hear you saying it looks a bit like this ... [*Counsellor does his own drawing, speaking as he is doing it, and puts it alongside Ken's drawing.*] What shall we call your drawing?

KEN: The Promise.

COUNSELLOR: OK. It is 'The Promise'. How about writing that on it somewhere, Ken?

KEN: I will, in this corner in big letters ... I want to do some more drawings and things like this again.

COUNSELLOR: That's right, Ken. There are other drawings to be made ... Let's find another ... What do you say we find one right now?

In using language, clients are actively perceiving, talking about themselves, creating meaning, trying to make sense of their world: their situations, problems, aspirations and experiences. Clients communicate internally to themselves and externally to the counsellors. All this communicating is done by selective filtering of the world in which the client lives. In NLP counselling it is therefore useful to regard the client as using their brain as a selection mechanism for understanding their world. Clients can only attend to particular aspects of their experience at any one time and over time. We believe they do this through a process of selecting and filtering information from their environment.

> The suggestion is that the function of the brain and nervous system and sense organs is in the main eliminative and not productive. Each person is at each moment capable of remembering all that has ever happened to him and of perceiving everything that is happening in the universe. The function of the brain and nervous system is to protect us from being overwhelmed and confused by this mass of largely useless and irrelevant knowledge, by shutting most of what we should otherwise perceive or remember at any moment, and leaving only that very small and special selection which is likely to be practically useful.
>
> (CD Broad)

Language: the Bridge Between the Client and the NLP Counsellor

●

Language, as we understand it, acts like a bridge between the client and the NLP counsellor. This means being aware of what language clients use and how they use it during counselling sessions. Language is the filter through which we express our experience to one another. We need to know which words are included and excluded by clients and the tonality, emphasis, pace, feelings, thoughts and behaviours that go along with them. We need to know what meaning their language has for clients.

Equally important for the NLP counsellor is discovering the structure of language used by clients and the processes which underpin the expressions of language in counselling. When we know the structure and process that lead to the language used by clients in counselling we have found the key to helping them choose and change.

The Processes of Deletion, Distortion & Generalization

In NLP counselling clients engage in deletion, distortion and generalization to manage the internal and external information they receive and filter through their senses. In practical terms, clients use these processes to make the best choices available to them to live their lives in the best way they know.

DELETION

Clients are using deletion when they selectively attend to particular aspects of their experience while ignoring other aspects that may or may not be present. A 20-year-old man comes to you for counselling. He is anxious. He tells you his mother never says any nice things about him any more. Yet when you visit him at home, his mother says to him how pleased she is that he has found a job and that he has a friend to share a rented flat. The man had deleted such compliments, although they were made by his mother. In this case, using deletion was unhelpful to the man and his relationship with his mother, but it is not always unhelpful when counselling clients.

A typical example where people use deletion is when they are travelling in an aeroplane. By using deletion to ignore recent stories about air crashes, passengers feel less vulnerable and do not suffer from fear or phobias about flying. Using deletion can be an unwise or a wise and useful choice for clients in NLP counselling. The lesson for the counsellor is clear. We should not encourage or discourage the use of deletion. What is required is for us to learn whether or not the client is using deletion in a way that is appropriate for them. A general rule for the counsellor is to ask the question: Is this person's use of deletion providing them with the experience they desire? If it is not then deletion is inappropriate for the client and in choosing to use deletion they are creating their own personal problems or at the very least adding to them.

DISTORTION

The same can be said for clients who are using distortion to manage or resolve their problems or a particular experience in their lives. As with deletion, using distortion may be a wise choice for a client, but it can also be used to cope with a real threat to their well-being and even their survival. Suppose a client in counselling is facing a major operation. The chances of the operation being a success are slim. The client has been given this rather grim news by her surgeon on a number of occasions. The client tells her surgeon that she has understood what he had to say, but when you ask the client what it means to her, she tells you that she has good prospects of coming successfully through the operation and taking up a normal life within a few months. The client is indicating her use of distortion in changing the message she gives to others about her physical health. On top of this, she may have distorted the message for herself, as this is better for her to hear than the one she was given by the surgeon.

A traumatized client who had been the victim of a bank raid said she could not bear the sound of the robber's voice. It made her shake with fear. It came back to her time and time again during the day. She could not sleep at night. When she went back to the bank she said she could hear the sound of his horrible crackly voice banging in her ears. Now the counsellor knew that the client loved the opera and was enthralled by Puccini's works. She was encouraged to gradually work through the bank raid again, up to the moment when the robber started making demands for money. This time, though, she was to have the robber sing out his demands in the form of one of her favourite arias. Once she had done this several times, and repeated the process during the day outside the counselling session and before going to bed, she overcame her fear and slept much better at night. In this case the NLP counsellor deliberately encouraged the client to use distortion for her therapeutic benefit.

GENERALIZATION

Most children who have once had their fingers burnt by touching a hot stove will not do it again. They do not have to repeat the experience. They learn through generalization. This is learning once and for all. We all use generalization as an efficient way of running our lives. Without appropriate use of generalization, we would soon discover that life could become very confusing. For instance, if we were to pull at a door that says 'push', or if we were to provide answers first and then ask the corresponding questions, we would find ourselves in great difficulty. These rather absurd examples testify to the extensive use of generalization in human psychology and behaviour.

Language itself has generalizations built into it. In English, terms such as 'always', 'forever', 'never', 'absolutely', 'whenever', 'nobody' and 'everybody' are generalizations. Clients naturally use generalizations in their spoken language within and outside counselling sessions. For instance, you ask a client to describe their problem to you. They may reply by telling you they have always had headaches. They never go away. Another client may say that, whenever they go out with their friends, they end up fighting and rowing with each other. Always, never, whenever — just three ways in which clients structure their experience by using generalization.

Generalization can be enabling. It can also be disabling. One of the most striking examples of the disabling use of generalization is the client who complains of phobia: an irrational fear of harmless circumstances or situations. A famous case showed how a little boy was very frightened if he got too near furry objects. It all started when he experienced a loud bang just as he was about to touch and play with a pet rabbit. Soon he was frightened of any rabbit and he then extended his use of generalization further to be fearful of many other things that had fur on them or were furry in their appearance. In NLP terms he was applying a model of generalizing to the class of objects referred to as 'furry'. He learned to use this model to produce a fearful response. Unfortunately it was inappropriate and created a phobic response to otherwise benign circumstances. His therapy, using counter-conditioning, was successful. He was given little pieces of chocolate as he got nearer and nearer to a rabbit and was eventually able to touch it again. His phobic responses to other fur-related objects disappeared.

From an NLP perspective we would say that the little boy was able to regeneralize his new model of reactions to the world of furry things and create a relaxed or pleasurable response to them. In our NLP counselling we have successfully practised similar principles with many phobic clients. In these instances we lead clients to build different generalizations about their world.

PARADOXICAL EFFECTS OF CHOOSING

We have noticed a curious thing about clients who use deletion, distortion and generalization. It can create a paradoxical effect for them. On the one hand, by engaging in these processes, clients often make it possible to cope with life and survive in the world. On the other, these processes may limit the choices available to clients. Clients choose what they become and they become what they choose. In making these choices they consciously or unconsciously filter in and out the information that creates their experience of reality. NLP counsellors need to tune their ears to hearing when clients are using deletion, distortion and generalization in creating language descriptions of their problems.

Listening
●

We would urge you not to just use an NLP 'cook-book' approach to listening when you are counselling clients. First and foremost, we should learn to listen to clients and what they have to say about themselves, their relationships and their concerns. Listening has a special place in NLP counselling. As with other forms of listening in counselling, it is important that NLP counsellors listen with respect. And it is often useful if clients perceive that they are being listened to and respected by counsellors. Listening also entails hearing what is said and checking that with the client, using reflective listening and summarizing, offering feedback and asking the client if we have understood them. If not, we need to ask clients if they can help us to better understand them and what they need and want out of their lives. Listening also means using our eyes as well as our ears. Listening in this sense is broader in that, as NLP counsellors, we are 'listening' with all of our senses and feelings in order that we can learn about the client and from the client. Our listening in NLP counselling therefore includes empathic listening. We listen to and with the client. We learn to listen and we listen to learn.

Counselling with NLP requires us to have all of these practical counselling skills, but NLP counsellors tend to use more directive than non-directive counselling. This means we are listening *for* specific patterns and the clients' use of sensory representation in their accounts of their experiences and problems. What, then, is the NLP counsellor specifically listening for?

Listening for Deletion, Distortion and Generalization

When we are counselling with NLP we are particularly listening for the way clients use deletion, distortion and generalization that arise from the sensory representations they make to create their experiences. More specifically, we are listening for the way clients describe their problems and their relationships with others and the particular contexts within which their problems occur. How this is done is fascinating. Bandler and Grinder showed that, as well as processing information from sensory representation of reality, clients predicate their descriptions in a similar way.

PREDICATES IN NLP COUNSELLING

Predicates in NLP counselling are the words or phrases which clients utilize to communicate their thinking, feelings, behaviour and experience to the counsellor, to describe their model of the world. They also reveal the sensory modality that is being used by clients at any particular time (see Table 2).

Table 2: Typical language predicates used by clients and their associated sensory representational system		
Visual predicates	**Auditory predicates**	**Kinaesthetic predicates**
imagine	talk through	hold on
focus	tune in	put finger on
look at	listen to	strikes me
point out	rings a bell	touched me
seeing it	explain it	numbed by
notice	crashing down	get a grip of
show it	deaf to	walk away
blind to	harmony	dragging me down
visualize	smashing me up	in touch with
in a flash	harsh tone	out of touch with
review	discord	unfeeling
an eyeful	an earful	a handful
I see/don't see	outspoken	caught in the act
picture	a listening ear	underhanded
bright as day	shrill manner	close-fisted
dark as night	squeaky clean	touchy subject
transparent	calling me	tingling
graphically	a little voice	sensation
illustrate	hear me out	sticking to/with
brilliant	sounding off	firm stance
viewpoint	jangling chatter	no stomach for it
drawing a blank	music to my hears	chilling thought
like a snapshot	keep telling myself	the weight of the world
like a movie	lowering the tone	hanging on

TRANSLATING PREDICATES TO MATCH CLIENT REPRESENTATIONAL SYSTEMS

We have found consistently that one of the things clients most want is to be understood. In NLP this means understanding their internal world — what we call the client map. Being able to translate the predicates used by clients and match these with the particular sensory representational system in use helps us to understand clients better. It also helps them to appreciate that they are understood. Mutual understanding helps to create rapport and trust between counsellors and clients. It can also provide the information upon the basis of which client change may take place.

In the two excerpts that follow, taken from NLP counsellors and their clients, see if you can spot the predicate words and phrases used by the clients.

Counsellor-Client Exchange One

COUNSELLOR: Neil, I am glad you could come to today ... Last time, you said that you wanted to make some changes in your life. What has happened since we last met?

NEIL: Well, not a lot ... I have drawn a blank really ... I mean, I have decided to make changes — I need to, otherwise my wife will leave me ... but I seem to have a blind spot ... I mean, I would like to show her ... I could change ... but ...

COUNSELLOR: But you haven't got a clear idea yet about that.

NEIL: No. I can't imagine how to begin ... but I do want to .... I want to strike out in a different direction today ... that's what I want from this session.

COUNSELLOR: OK. Let's take a closer look at what you want and how you might get hold of it.

Counsellor-Client Exchange Two

COUNSELLOR: Meg, how would you describe your situation now?

MEG: I suppose I can best explain it to you like this ... I have tried talking over how jealous I get with Chris ... my partner ... but he doesn't seem to want to hear what I have to say ... so much of the time we aren't tuned into each other much these days ... there is a huge silent gulf between us. [*She starts to cry.*] I'm sorry, I sound awful whingy ...

COUNSELLOR: You know, Meg, as I am sitting here listening to you I wonder what it might be like if you and Chris were more tuned into each other.

MEG: Mmm ... for a start ... we could talk things over ... We haven't ... spoken for three weeks now ...

COUNSELLOR: And before the last three weeks — you can tell me something about that ... can you not?

MEG: Oh, then we were really in harmony with each other — you know ... playing music and having a good time.

COUNSELLOR: And then something happened that brought discord into your life ...

MEG: Yes ... yes ... Chris's ex-wife turned up and ruined everything ... She caused the clash between us ... The sound of her voice makes me so mad I just boil up inside and want to smash something ... My heart hurts ... I think it might burst ... and ...

Using Predicates and the Language Modalities

●

The next time you are working with a client in a counselling session take a few moments to notice the number of predicates they are using, the kind of predicates and the frequency of some in particular. You will be surprised to find out how often we and our clients are predicating what we say, rather like Molière's bourgeois gentilhomme, who was speaking prose all the time, but did not know it. The task for the NLP counsellor is to utilize the clients' use of predicates and introduce them into the service of the counselling session (see Table 3).

Table 3: Examples of client predicating and NLP counsellor responses	
Client	**Counsellor**
It's no use, I can't see a way out	You are in a blind alley
All I can see is a dark cloud	You have lost sight of the blue sky
This smells like dead fish	There is an odour of decay about you
I hear his voice every day	The sound of his voice is with you

Sensory Systems, Predicates and Submodalities

●

Communicating with clients involves being aware of the sensory systems they are utilizing at each moment they are talking with the counsellor. It also requires us to know which predicates are being used to describe the problems and concerns clients say they have. We have seen how this can involve the 4-tuple and the meaning of language for each client. More than this, each client can use a wide range of submodalities to communicate her experiences to the counsellor and the NLP counsellor can accept these descriptions to move the counselling process in the way that allows the client to make the most of the choices available to her. How do we do this? First we need to notice the main client submodalities and adapt our counsellor responses to them. We can then create opportunities for talking to clients and working with them to limit information to that which is useful for changes they may wish to make in their lives.

Limiting information is necessary for our good mental health, but it is also responsible for many of the problems that clients present to counsellors in counselling. Once we know how clients are using language and the way they are constructing their world we can speak their language fluently. The purpose of language in

NLP counselling is to be at the centre of what counsellors use to create the conditions for client change. We are reminded of a useful conundrum for counsellors. In *Alice's Adventures in Wonderland*, the March Hare advises Alice: 'Then you must say what you mean ..." "I do," Alice hastily replied; "at least — I mean what I say — that's the same thing, you know."

We must understand the language of clients, but in NLP counselling we need to go beyond the content of what is said by clients to the structure of their experience. As counsellors we are interested in the language which clients use to produce meaning and the meanings inferred consciously or habitually by them in counselling: language has personal significance for clients. For us it encompasses the language used by clients as well as the symbolic meaning it has for them.

Talking with Clients
●

If you had a video of an NLP counselling session you would see a lot, hear a lot and have feelings about what you see and hear. The client would be talking and so would the NLP counsellor. As you can see from our earlier case examples, conversations with clients take many forms. Sometimes they are like a river — they seem to flow along and find their own level, and they twist and turn, speed up and slow down, just like the currents in a river. Occasionally the river is in full spate and the conversation is flooded by a surge of words, emotions, tonalities and feelings. At other times the river hardly seems to move on the surface; all seems calm, but underneath there are undercurrents pulling the client and counsellor towards an as yet unknown destination. Some conversations become like a stagnant lake and dry up. And there are conversations more like canals, with clear boundaries and rules of navigation on how to get from one psychological state to another. The counsellor has the task of sharing in staying afloat and utilizing the movements and inertia in the conversations with clients.

Counsellor and client learn to talk to each other in a way that leads them to their destination. In NLP terms, talking with clients has many purposes, among them to create and sustain rapport, and to obtain information. Once there is sufficient information the client and counsellor can move towards the choices they can make which may take them to the state they wish to experience. When they have achieved this they have obtained their outcome for the particular counselling session or therapeutic contract they have agreed. Information is the key the NLP counsellor uses to unlock future client choices.

Chapter 5

REACHING OUT THROUGH RAPPORT

The State of Rapport

●

In NLP we describe rapport as the counsellor's ability to respond symmetrically to the client's model of the world. At any one time rapport can be understood as a specific state existing between client and counsellor. One immediate task, therefore, is for NLP counsellors to use the appropriate counselling skills with their clients which create and maintain rapport.

Without a state of rapport between counsellors and clients the processes of counselling can break down. We would go so far as to say that counselling cannot take place without rapport. Rapport is the concrete that binds the process of helping people change together. Counselling without rapport is like building a house on weak foundations. It breaks up very quickly. It will not serve its purpose for very long. To stay the course of counselling, we would urge NLP counsellors to be conscious of pursuing a fundamental task with their clients: creating, recreating and maintaining a state of robust rapport.

Creating Rapport in NLP Counselling

●

Creating rapport is something which is shared by many counselling approaches to help people change. However, in NLP counselling the counsellor takes an active role in creating the conditions whereby clients may choose to change themselves, their situation or their map of reality. Creating rapport in NLP counselling has three interrelated parts.

1 The NLP counsellor *actively* initiates and pursues the creation of rapport with clients: this is one of his essential tasks.
2 The NLP counsellor must know how rapport is created and broken and to be able to utilize the skills he has to create rapport with *any* client.
3 Sometimes clients have been blamed for the failure to achieve rapport in counselling and psychotherapy. In these cases clients are described as being 'resistant' or 'defensive' or as expressing 'transference problems'. None of this makes sense to an NLP counsellor. The NLP counsellor has the responsibility to create rapport with all clients in counselling. This may appear a tall order, but it should not be. It all depends on what the clients bring into their counselling sessions. In NLP counselling rapport is built 'from the ground upwards'. The NLP counsellor *does not* have a fixed precept for the way rapport will have to be built. He needs be much more flexible in approaching the creation of rapport with clients in counselling.

The Purpose of Rapport
●

Building rapport is not a matter of meeting to have a cosy chat. Most counsellors achieve rapport rapidly with clients, but for some this is where counselling begins and ends. In NLP counselling rapport has a special place, a particular purpose. Rapport is created to serve the purposes of NLP counselling, which are to create the conditions whereby clients may choose to change and find new and interesting ways to carry out these changes in their lives. To do this we need to be able to do more than know how to create and build rapport with clients. We need to look and listen and feel for ways to join them in their experience, pace alongside them and lead them to consider their choices and how they might alter their maps of reality.

Joining the Client

●

The first part of building rapport is joining the client. This simply means meeting them within their own frame of reference as they approach counselling. Creating lasting rapport depends on the NLP counsellor using joining skills that last and bond them strongly with their clients.

Joining Skills

You can join the client in many different ways: in the kinds of language they use; the way they form their words; the tone; the particular pauses and emphases in their speech that they adopt when talking about certain problems. These are all opportunities for joining clients. You can join them even before you meet them in the counselling room. We often use the phone to join clients and lay the solid grounds for rapport and future work with them. When a client rings and says her name, you say your own and ask how you might be able to help. You can say this in different ways: welcoming, disapproving, uncertain. Our voice tells the client how she is being received.

Fortunately joining is not dependent on the counsellor or therapist. The information we need for joining clients in counselling comes from the client. So a client who phones and sounds annoyed should find that the NLP counsellor or therapist also uses a slightly irritated tone during their conversation. In NLP counselling adopting a similar tone, pitch and volume to our clients' greatly helps to establish and maintain rapport. The days when counselling involved indiscernible grunts and bland verbalizations are gone. Or at least they should be. Not every client likes being grunted at or made the target of irrelevant assurances by the counsellor.

Joining is important in NLP counselling for another reason: Rejoining. Rejoining is necessary every time after the first counselling session. When you have had a bad first counselling session, making a mess of joining the client, you start all over again. When joining has been successful, so will rejoining be. You will know it and the client will know it. Subsequent NLP counselling progresses more satisfactorily when sufficient attention is paid to joining the client. Unsuccessful joining and overhasty counselling often inhibit the client participating actively in initial contact and future counselling sessions. Novice counsellors sometimes have an excessive zeal to reach the client and start working on their problems, at the expense of paying attention to joining the client.

Initial joining creates a memory for future joining. This is why we would encourage you to spend time thinking of the many ways you can join your clients as you collaborate in the activity of NLP counselling. Observe people and notice how they join each other in different ways and how this contributes to their rapport or lack of it. For instance, see how people in a bus queue join each other temporarily but then disperse quickly as soon as they move onto the bus. In a bar you can spot the people who are going to be in deep rapport with each other by the way they join each other. See how they meet and greet each other. Do they have similar movements? What is the pitch and tone of their voices? At first it may not matter what they actually say to each other — it is the initial rapport which you look for when you study joining.

In the past counsellors have described counselling as a special kind of communication between two people. On a very general level this can be said to be one of the truisms of counselling. Communication plays a big part in the counselling process and in enhancing rapport, but it is important to be clear that communication in counselling involves much more than the words we actually utter. Words are only a small part of what goes on in the expressive encounter we call counselling. Otherwise all the counsellor would have to do would be to tell the client what to do to get better and they would do it.

A revealing piece of social research in communication by the psychologist Michael Argyle and his colleagues confirms our view that counselling is more than the sum of words exchanged between clients and counsellors. Argyle showed that, in a presentation given to a group of people, 55 per cent of what was communicated was determined by body language, 38 per cent by the tone of voice and only 7 per cent of what was communicated depended on what was actually said! In other words our posture, mannerisms, eye contact and gestures, followed by our voice tonality, play a highly significant part in the way our words are expressed and received. Just think for a moment about the different ways you can say 'Hello' or 'Good morning' to a client and you can understand that it can be welcoming, threatening or hostile, intolerant or inviting to them. Try it for yourself now: say 'Good morning' or 'Hello' in as many different ways as possible to a colleague or friend and then ask them how they experienced what you communicated to them. In NLP counselling, the meaning of any communication is the way it is received by the client and not the way it is intended by the counsellor. Once we can accept this, it becomes clear how important joining is in developing and maintaining rapport in counselling sessions with clients.

As we are reminded in song, 'It's not what you say it's the way that you say it ... it's not what you do it's the way that you do it ... that's what gets results.'

Clearly, then, it is not counsellor intention that is important in NLP counselling but the clients' experience of our attempts to join them and create rapport with them. The long-running television programmes that we call 'soap operas' have a great deal to teach us about joining and creating rapport. Why are they so successful? One reason is that they subtly but deliberately create and achieve joining with their viewing audiences. We believe this forms the basis for future viewing and loyalty to the programme. The accents and movements used by the actors mirror the way their viewers actually behave or would like to. Perhaps the extreme example of this is when we start to talk like the actors we see in the programme and adopt 'their' mannerisms, sayings and attitudes.

Matching and Mirroring
●

Much of what we do to build rapport with clients involves matching and mirroring. When we are matching we are copying movements made by the client. For instance, a client may cough and a few seconds later the counsellor clears his throat, producing a cough of his own. When we are mirroring we imitate client movements by producing a similar movement but by using the reverse side and part of the body. Let us say that a client starts pointing with their left hand; the NLP counsellor could adopt a similar gesture with their right hand. The point of matching and mirroring is to create rapport, not to be an obvious 'copycat' of the client. Matching and mirroring can be very subtle and need not always involve gross and blatant imitating of what the client is doing. However, even when clients are aware of the counsellor matching and mirroring their movements, gestures and tone of voice, and ideas and selected words, we find they do not object or find it offensive. Most of the time, though, clients have too many concerns, problems and worries, to be aware of the matching and mirroring activity of the counsellor.

Matching and mirroring help to create rapport, and rapport fosters trust. Trust is not something that should happen accidentally in NLP counselling. After all, there is no reason whatsoever why clients should trust a counsellor. The counsellor has to earn the trust. They have to build it. Opening up the gateway to trust is done through vigilantly creating, building and sustaining rapport. For us, reaching out and achieving rapport hinges on subtle and accurate matching and mirroring with each client. It is used for joining the client, pacing them through counselling sessions and leading them towards choices and changes in their lives.

Body Postures and Movements

Adopting similar body postures and movements is a sure sign that people are in rapport. Have you noticed how people who meet and like each other tend to lean closer together or the way friends who drink together raise their drinks and drink them almost at the same time? Lovers and romancing couples also use similar postures or movements in a sign of deep rapport: putting heads together, looking in each other's eyes, leaning against each other and stroking each other are all indicative of shared rapport.

In NLP counselling sessions we need to be aware of the body postures and movements adopted by clients and how we can join them in building rapport. There are quite a number we have noticed that are immediately amenable to matching and mirroring that can help to lead us into instant rapport with clients. See if you agree with those we have listed in Table 4 and add some of your own. Decide how you would specifically match and mirror your body movements with those of the client. Once you know, practise body posture matching and mirroring with your clients and notice what happens to the rapport between you.

Table 4: Body postures and movements	
Client body postures/ movements	**Counsellor matching/mirroring**
sits upright on couch	sits upright on chair
leans to right on couch arm	leans on own arm to left
legs stretched out	arms slightly stretched out
left leg straight/right leg bent	left leg straight/right leg bent
arms crossed across chest	left arm crossed across chest, right arm resting on right leg
arms folded left over right	wrists folded right over left
left arm hangs and dangles down to left	leans to the left
head central, hung forwards and looking down at floor	head central, hung forwards and looking at spot knee-high
head cocked to the left	head cocked to the left
head cocked to the right	head cocked to the right
head cocked to the right	head cocked to the left
runs fingers of left hand through hair	runs fingers of right hand through beard
runs fingers of right hand through hair	runs fingers of left hand along left arm of chair
twists and curls hair under left ear with right hand	rolls thumb against first two fingers of right hand
talks in a whisper	speaks in a quiet voice
grimaces before speaking	grimaces and then listens
grimaces before asking a question	grimaces before answering
pats chin and looks down	taps top of hand with fingers

The Limits of Mind-Reading

Counsellors should not jump to conclusions about clients simply on the strength of their presuppositions about client body language. Just because we know what the postures and movements of clients are, we should not confuse this with 'mind-reading' and erroneously infer that specific postures and body movements 'mean' that the client is in a particular state. Body postures and movements provide the NLP counsellor with information; information that the client will work with and which the counsellor can utilize in creating the conditions where clients may choose to change or not to change. Information about body postures and movements does not represent a simple equation of body language that is interpreted by the counsellor as always having a particular meaning. Of course body postures and movements make a fundamental contribution to the process of helping people change in counselling, but in NLP counselling the task, the excitement and challenge, for the counsellor and client, lie in discovering what significance body postures *may or may not* have in counselling each individual client, each pair or group. We have found it is sometimes far too easy to judge the posture and body movements of clients and their meaning for the clients too soon and *to get it wrong*!

Client body movements and postures have meaning, certainly, but for the client. This is what the NLP counsellor continually needs to remind himself of when working with clients. It is his task to discover with clients the meaning of their movements and the significance they may have in maintaining or resolving their adduced problems.

Hand and Finger Movements in Rapport

We can add to the vast range of body postures. We can match and mirror to build rapport by paying attention to our clients' hand and finger movements. We find that our clients' hands and fingers are often very busy in the counselling sessions. They provide wonderful opportunities for matching, mirroring and building and maintaining rapport. The hands and fingers of clients can be quite dead and lifeless or lively and animated for long periods during counselling sessions. There is an interesting story that illustrates just how important the hands can be in NLP counselling.

THE FARMER AND HIS WIFE

Once there was a young farmer who had a little money to buy much-needed seed for his survival and the security of his wife and family. He had big pressures and big problems. He did not know how to make a decision about sowing seed in a particular plot of land. He thought and thought about where he should sow the seed. He pondered how much seed he should sow and he spent many hours worrying about the right kind of seed to buy that would be strong and grow in the stony soil as well as in the rich loam of the land.

One night when he was in the depths of despair he noticed that both of his hands were clenched tight into fists, so great were the tension and worry he was experiencing. Just as he was about to give up his struggle to overcome his difficulties, he noticed that his wife was sitting next to him and her hands were closed tight like his. He looked at her hands and then at his own with rapid fleeting glances. He repeated this several times, his eyes flicking to and fro like a pendulum going back and forth on a clock. Then his wife did something special. She slowly opened one hand — one finger at a time — and then the other. And do you know what? The farmer did the same.

That night he had the best sleep in weeks. The next day he went straight to the market and ran his hands through the different buckets of grain, lifting and smelling it from time to time. At last he came to a barrel and immediately decided to buy the grain in it. The grain he bought gave him a wonderful harvest. Later he was asked how he managed to make the decision and choose so well. He said all he could remember was that his wife had helped him, but he did not know how. But now he was able to trust his hands and his nose to make decisions for him in the future, instead of sitting at home and worrying.

Voice Tonality and Breathing Patterns

The tone of voice and breathing patterns are useful in creating rapport with clients. The client who has a high-pitched voice and breathes high in the chest can be matched and mirrored by the NLP counsellor. Similarly clients who have deeper voices or emphasize specific tonalities when describing themselves, their concerns, their situations and their families can also be matched and mirrored to create and maintain rapport in counselling sessions. We have found that those clients who have deeper voices tend to breathe from their abdomen, in a more rhythmical way. Next time you are counselling a client notice their voice tonality at different points in the session and the breathing patterns that accompany the voice tonality they are using. Pay particular attention to the way your client's voice tonality and breathing change when they talk about the different problems they say they are experiencing in their lives. The breathing of one client who was describing her family was quite regular, rhythmical and relaxed and she spoke in even tones until she came to describe her younger daughter, when she said in an emphatic way, "My younger daughter." At this point the tonality had changed and so had her breathing. The NLP counsellor noticed these changes and changed his own breathing and tonality to match the client's. After this the counsellor commented on these changes and asked the client if she had noticed what was going on in her experience as she described the younger daughter. The client said that, for the first time, someone had spotted the uneasiness she felt when talking about this member of the family.

Voice tonality and breathing patterns are often closely associated with eye movements of clients and the extent to which they are retrieving memories or associations visually, auditorially or kinaesthetically.

Breathing from the diaphragm and a deep sonorous voice are often characteristic of clients who are kinaesthetic. We have found these clients are feeling a lot in their sessions. The NLP counsellor needs to know this in order to match and mirror breathing and voice tonality back to his clients. Those clients who tend to represent their reality through a feeling modality seem to develop better rapport when we reflect our feelings back to them. Clearly it is of little use for NLP counsellors to ask clients what they are thinking when they are in a feeling state. Doing this only threatens to break rapport — imperilling the very thing we are aiming to accomplish with the client.

It is similar with clients who represent their reality visually. The breathing of these clients, we find, is shallower and higher in their chests. Their tone of voice is often higher and lighter and their voice sounds 'thinner' than that of the kinaesthetic. Building rapport with these clients means raising our voices an octave or two when counselling and adopting a similar breathing pattern. Clients tending towards the auditory mode are inclined to breathe rhythmically and their voice tonality can have a wider and richer range of representation and emphasis when they are describing their problems and concerns in counselling.

Although clients may have preferred breathing and tonality patterns as well as particular ways in which they represent their realities through their different sensory systems, they are not bound to one, and only one. We need to remember the different ways in which clients use their voice tonality and breathing patterns. Reaching out to them and building satisfactory rapport depends on this. When we observe a specific pattern of breathing, when we notice a typical voice pattern and tonality, we can establish lasting rapport with clients. The important point is to notice what is happening in our work with clients in NLP counselling, because this provides us with a rich source of reliable client feedback. It is client feedback which forms the raw information upon which rapport and NLP counselling are based. Clearly there are many types of feedback from clients. However, the task for the NLP counsellor is to discover the *individual map of each client* and the specific model of *their* world which makes up their experience.

Avoiding the Stereotyping Fallacy
●

In counselling, we believe we need to be vigilant in observing the different as well as the typical patterns used by clients. Deep and lasting rapport can be damaged and even broken if we do not make this a focal point of our NLP counselling and put it into practice. Otherwise we run the risk of committing what we describe as the stereotyping fallacy. A few examples will illustrate the point.

► A client who has red hair is thought to be quick-tempered.

► A client born rich tends to be seen as confident and superior.

► A fat client is assumed to be happy and easy-going.

► A person labelled an 'alcoholic' is considered to be a cheat.

► A women client who goes to bars on her own is 'asking for trouble'.

► Bald men who are clients are thought to be perverse and promiscuous.

► A client who has attended public school is perceived as being latently homosexual or sadistic.

These are just some examples of the stereotyping fallacy. They are useful only when they confirm what clients say about themselves, or when they behave in a way that confirms the stereotype. Otherwise they are worthless and counsellors should avoid committing the stereotyping fallacy with clients because of the danger of ruining rapport and any hope of real and lasting change with clients. Stereotyping narrows clients' choice — their right to choose who they are, what they say, do, think and feel.

How does the stereotyping fallacy apply in NLP counselling? Stereotyping can be subtle — it is not always crude or obvious — and this is when it is at its most dangerous and limiting to counsellors and clients alike. Stereotyping can occur very early in NLP counselling. Consider the examples below (Table 5) of the stereotyping fallacy in NLP counselling. When you have studied them, think of situations where they could occur and how you could overcome the risks involved. Write down any other forms of stereotyping you can think of and keep them as reminders of things to avoid. Also keep them fresh in your mind and be receptive to them in your work with clients when you are building rapport using NLP counselling.

The stereotyping fallacy is easy to fall into. We have done it ourselves and sometimes still do at unreflective and uncritical moments in our practice — a good reason for scheduling regular supervision with an NLP counsellor supervisor.

Counsellors new to NLP counselling may also fall into the trap of stereotyping clients. It is interesting to hear graduates from NLP training courses talking: he is a kino; she is a visualizer; that one is audio. These are good signs if they have learned to

Table 5: Examples of the stereotyping fallacy in NLP counselling	
Client	**Stereotyping fallacy**
client looks down to the right	counsellor always refers to the client as a 'kino' type and fails to notice other ways she represents her experience
client looks up and left and then to right and down and then up left again	counsellor only notices the first eye movements, then talks in visual terms, assuming the client is always in visual mode
clients' eyes flick from side to side at one point in the session	immediately the counsellor categorizes them as 'audios'
client who has difficulty in speaking because of personal trauma and is blocked off from her feelings or thoughts	counsellor wrongly assumes client is a 'kino' and keeps asking how she 'feels'
client says she cannot see a way out of her problem/ situation	counsellor incorrectly infers the client is a visualizer and encourages her to visualize more

understand aspects of client eye accessing to and sensory representations of reality, but bad if they fall foul of the stereotyping fallacy in NLP counselling.

We have mentioned the stereotyping fallacy here simply as a caution to those students, trainers and therapists who are seriously interested in NLP counselling. It is essential that we do not fall into the seductive trap of stereotyping clients. First, it limits our perception of them. Second, it may limit clients' perception of themselves. Third, and particularly pertinent from an NLP perspective, it may limit the range of rapport-building skills we bring to counselling sessions with clients. Type, but almost never stereotype, is a useful rule in reaching out, joining and building durable rapport with clients.

Reaching out to clients is our attempt to connect with them as people. To do this we need to be resourceful and skilful in building robust and lasting rapport. The ancient Taoist saying that the longest journey begins with the first step is pertinent to our understanding of the central importance of rapport in NLP counselling. When we connect with clients in NLP counselling we have taken the first significant steps on our journey through counselling with them. Matching and mirroring helps the counsellor to help the client. And the client helps the counsellor to know which steps they may take together on their journey in, through and out of counselling. Matching and mirroring body movements and postures and avoiding stereotyping are ways that help us to gain a sure footing and not end up in too many blind alleys. Having taken our first steps with clients we have started to share the beginning of a common language in counselling. We have begun to learn how to talk to each other.

Chapter 6

APPLYING INTELLIGENCE AND UTILIZING PERSONAL INFORMATION

Doing the Best We Can

●

Our approach to client counselling with NLP assumes a simple but profound truth about applying our intelligence and the information we have available to us. At any time, in any place, with anyone and in any way, we are doing the best we can. We believe this truism is applicable to counsellors as well as clients in NLP counselling. We would like to spend a little time explaining why we hold this belief.

We have found that clients come to counselling having tried many ways to overcome their personal problems and private pain. They have tried deep relaxation and assertiveness training; they have been involved in anger management training; they have worked on themselves and attended group sessions in counselling. Many of our clients have benefited from these and other forms of counselling and psychotherapy; some have not; and a few have been damaged more as a result of their experiences at the hands of so-called, self-styled 'counsellors'. We can think of the woman who attended a counselling clinic and seemed to be getting nowhere until she built up enough courage to let the counsellor know that she felt isolated and lonely. In floods of tears, she told the counsellor what had happened to her at the hands of another therapist. She had been exposed to a form of 'silent' counselling in which the therapist did not speak to her for the entire session, and this went on once a week for six months. Apparently the therapeutic idea — if we can call it that — was that the client should 'get in touch' with her deeper self and her guilt and shame, 'to put her in touch with reality'. All it served to do was brutalize and humiliate her and further undermine her already belittled sense of self-worth.

We use this example only as a way of making some elementary points. First of all, the client in question did the best she could. She found a counsellor. She sought and found a place where she could engage in some form of counselling. She used the information she had available to her at the time. She did the best she could up to a certain point where she withdrew from the counselling sessions being offered to her. As for the therapist involved, presumably he believed that he was doing the best that he could for the client. He practised a particular form of therapy. It did not work for the client we are discussing here and it may not have worked for others.

The outcome for the client was she left that counselling clinic and, after a period of reflection, personal pain and further thought, she searched for and found another counsellor at another clinic where she seemed to gain the kind of counselling which for her was more appropriate. This example illustrates the fact that clients and counsellors may not always get the right kind of counselling at the right time and in the right place. Nevertheless they are doing the best they can. At each moment they are in the process of solving what they regard as their problems.

Applying Intelligence
●

When clients and NLP counsellors are doing the best they can, they are applying their intelligence as best they know how to move from their present state to their desired state. What mental abilities are involved? As the psychologist Sternberg has recently argued, applying our intelligence means enlisting our mental abilities, which comprise a series of components and processes, in an effort to solve problems. He has classified these as shown in Table 6, and we believe they should be of great interest to anyone involved in NLP counselling.

Table 6: Classifying mental abilities	
Components	**Processes**
Metacomponents	Higher-order control processes used for executive planning and decision making in problem solving
Performance components	Processes that execute the plans and implement the decisions selected by metacomponents
Acquisition components	Processes involved in learning new information
Retention components	Processes involved in retrieving information previously stored in memory
Transfer components	Processes involved in carrying over retained information from one situation to another

Source: Adapted from Sternberg, quoted in Seigler (1991).

Case Example One: the Businesswoman

A 37-year-old businesswoman was anticipating an important appointment with a foreign buyer. She became anxious at the thought of not presenting her company in a favourable light. She came to a counselling clinic and said she wanted help. The NLP counsellor asked what she wanted most from the meeting. She said she needed to be calm and composed and know that she could appear confident in her communication with the buyer. The counsellor asked if she had conducted similar meetings in the past. She said she had and these had presented little difficulty for her; most of the meetings had gone very well.

Her counsellor said he was curious how she knew how to do the right thing at these past meetings and how she could feel good about them. She said she prepared for them well in advance and made a note of the key decisions she might have to face and the problems that would likely need attention in the meeting. The counsellor said that was good and asked what happened next. She said that as far as possible she put her plan into practice and carried out the decisions that came up with the problems in the meeting and, where she did face something unexpected, she would make arrangements to acquire the necessary information either before the meeting was over or to send it by 'fax' as soon as possible after the meeting. This, too, usually worked quite well.

The woman described herself in visual nominalizations and predicates, having feelings of competence and well-being at being able to achieve the purposes she set herself at past meetings. The counsellor then had a clear task. He worked with the businesswoman to 'get in touch' with those good feelings again and to rehearse visually how she would do exactly the same things with the foreign buyer who would be attending their business meeting. She felt very relaxed at the meeting. Later she reported to the counsellor, rather surprised, that 'it had gone very well'.

Case Example Two: the Student Who Could Not Finish

A 20-year-old psychology student who kept running out of time to complete university assignments came for counselling. He was asked by the NLP counsellor how he knew how to run out of time to complete his university assignments. At first the student seemed puzzled to be asked such a question. But after a few moments' reflection he said that he did know and it was easy for him to run out of time. The counsellor agreed and said to the student, "When you know how to do things, it's easy. You are especially good at running out of time; you don't even have to think about it — is that right?" The student spontaneously agreed with the counsellor. As can be imagined, by this time the student and the counsellor were in deep rapport. The counsellor was also using the same language predicates and a similar cognitive map to the student's.

Pursuing this process, the counsellor worked with the student to identify "what has to happen so well that sometimes we do not even have to think — we do things automatically". The student reasoned it must be like feeding ourselves and there must be some high-level processes in the brain that help us to organize feeding ourselves so that it is like an automatic plan: it just unfolds as soon as we make the decision to eat — we feed ourselves. The counsellor was still curious, so she asked the student, "But how could you make it happen so automatically?" The student explained that, since we learn to feed ourselves as babies and we remember how to do it, we can eat any time, anywhere, when we are hungry and food is available to us.

The counsellor then switched the attention of the student back to those situations where he ran out of time. The counsellor did this by asking the student to identify those specific situations in which he was 'good' at running out of time. The student made a short list with three items on it. They all involved projects and university assignments. The NLP counsellor wondered what the student had learned so far in their session. The student said that he now knew that he had a lot of abilities but some were so automatic that he had got into the habit of running out of time.

The counsellor then asked where in the course of the assignments and projects required time was not running away. Interestingly the student said that he had now learned that the start and middle stages of the project were not a problem but the last stages — the writing up of results and concluding his arguments — saw him running out of time. Here he began to feel very anxious, panicky and doubtful about his finishing abilities. At this point the counselling session headed in another direction and the counsellor was able to work with the student in rehearsing final stages of his projects and assignments in a state of relaxed, composed alertness. In this instance the counsellor also did more: she used the metaphor of feeding supplied by the student and combined this with using the fact that he was a student. At the conclusion of the session, she gave him an 'assignment': he could learn what he must feed himself to learn how to feel calm, composed and relaxed as he finished his university projects automatically. The session ended with the counsellor making a point of finding out from the student how much time it would take for him to digest the tasks the counsellor had set him.

Case Example Three: The Teenager Suffering from Post-traumatic Stress

A 16-year-old teenager called Tony, who was obsessed with computers, came to the counselling clinic suffering from post-traumatic stress. He had been harassed and bullied for a number of years by boys from his own school. Tony's favourite school subject was computing and information technology. He spent many hours engrossed in his subject. On his fourteenth birthday, Tony decided that he was fed up with the bullying and confronted the boys at school. Frighteningly for Tony, one of the boys had a knife and stabbed him several times in the back and sides of his body. Tony recovered from his physical injuries and moved to another part of the county and a different school. However he seemed unable to attend the new school even though bullying was dealt with severely and there was good discipline. Tony agreed to seek help from a counsellor.

When Tony came to counselling he would complain of being 'stressed-out' and break out into fits of shaking and trembling. He would also stammer on occasions and sometimes shout and swear when he recalled the events of the stabbing and how he had felt since then. He no longer went out on his own — day or night. If he did go out it was in the company of an adult and even then he became very anxious and insecure.

The NLP counsellor first worked with Tony to build a strong foundation of rapport and trust. After several sessions the counsellor congratulated Tony for managing to do the best he could with what for him must have been an awful, stressful experience. The NLP counsellor said that the stress, trembling and shaking, were all ways in which his body was giving him information that was intended to be useful. The counsellor added that the boys who bullied him and the one that stabbed him were all information that was intended to be useful for Tony.

Tony was asked if he could imagine that what had happened to him was a bit like running a computer program. Acknowledging that Tony was someone who was interested in computing, and who knew a lot about computers, the counsellor asked him to run through the information he had filed away that linked him up to the harassing, bullying and stabbing. Tony then arranged the information on those times and reported back to the counsellor. The counsellor reminded Tony how this information was just like the kind you programme into a computer. He thanked Tony for accessing his files about the stressful event and asked him to explain the program and how the events followed from the procedures he would describe. Tony then talked in great detail about the way certain decision points in such a program led up to his present experience. The NLP counsellor reminded Tony that it was just a program and asked, "What if we changed the procedures in a program on your computer files? What changes would be likely to happen?"

Tony now felt he was able to explain confidently to the counsellor that a program was 'only a program' and it could be changed 'and when you change it you get a different result'. The NLP counsellor agreed and emphasized to Tony by repeating to him, "Now Tony, is it not interesting how *your* program is *only* a program and by changing it you get a different result? That is right, isn't it, *you* get a different result?" Tony agreed and nodded, pleased that the counsellor apparently shared some of his personal map of reality. The next thing the counsellor did was wonderful. He asked Tony to sit 'progging' at his computer console the next day and work out a different program for the harassing and bullying and stabbing; he could choose how it would end differently and the changes that he would make in the beginning and the ending of his program. He also said, "Tony, you could use all the information you have and add more, or take some away or just enough to plan and decide how you would use old or new information to … so as to remember to do it differently." Tony was now highly motivated to do these tasks. To give him practice at producing his new 'personal program', the NLP counsellor offered Tony the opportunity of using the last 20 minutes of their session together to rehearse in his mind some of the changes he would make. Tony rehearsed some of the ways he would alter the information and the way he would reprogramme his recent traumatic experiences. He left the session calm, composed and in control of himself.

The Many Uses of Intelligence and Information

●

There are many obvious and not so obvious uses of intelligence and information in the three cases discussed above. What did you notice about the way practical intelligence was being employed by the counsellors and the clients in counselling? How was the personal information of the client used by the counsellor to build rapport and set an appropriate task for the client? Finally, were there other aspects of language and the use of metaphor deliberately introduced by the counsellors in their work with these clients? What were they? Why do you think they were utilized in the counselling process?

We can see these three cases as examples of the way we apply our higher-order intelligence to situations in the real world. The clients had to find a way of planning what they had to do and make important decisions about the problems they faced and how they might manage them. Beyond this, they needed to perform in the situation, carrying out the plan decisions and putting them into practice. Where there was insufficient information readily available to them, they had to acquire new information or find ways of gaining access to their memory and transfer the solutions they had available to the current situations they believed they faced and the problems they needed to solve. Doing this gives clients outcomes. Sometimes there will be an outcome they desire and sometimes they may experience an outcome which they do not desire. Whatever the outcome, it is unique to each client. The processes involved in applying our intelligence may be complex, but the result is simple though instructive. We either achieve our outcomes or we do not. Clients who come to NLP counselling are doing the best they can. They are applying their intelligence the best way they know how to achieve personal outcomes that they regard as being significant and important to them. They do this using the information that is available to them. Metaphorically, we can call this the information ocean.

The Information Ocean

Some clients simply lack information and, once they have access to personally significant information, they can organize appropriate plans and actions and make decisions to carry their actions out in specific situations. Most clients have an ocean of information at their disposal. One client may have a vast amount of readily accessible information from which they can select in order to solve their personal problems. Another may have a similar depth of information but not quite know how best to organize it or to plan solutions to problems. Others again have difficulty in retrieving information from their memories and transferring it or acting on it as solutions to their present problems. Such clients have a transfer of information problem as well as, say, suffering from anxiety. For if such clients could remember how they know how not to feel anxious and transfer this to the present situation they would not have a problem. They would not require counselling.

Why is this important for NLP counselling? First of all, it shows us that applying our intelligence is a wonderful way of using information in managing and overcoming our problems. Equally we can say that we apply our intelligence in diverse ways that can actually maintain or worsen our personal problems. We tend to perceive our clients as coming to counselling with an ocean of information to make new choices to overcome and change their lives available to them. Sometimes this ocean of information swamps them and they feel they are in danger of drowning. One task of the NLP counsellor is to help clients to learn to swim and ride the waves so as to make the most of the information they have available to them.

In NLP counselling, applying our intelligence depends on the personal information we have available to us and how it is put to use in specific situations at any one time. Clients may not always know the information they need or whether it is accessible. Or they may know the information they want to use but somehow need to reorganize it in such a way that they can put it to practical use and use their good sense to do so. This is one reason why clients seem troubled and in crisis, why they reach out to counsellors for help, in the earnest and sincere hope of comfort, cure, rehabilitation or recovery.

In NLP counselling we talk a great deal in metaphor with

clients. We like to point out that our clients know more about their problems than we do. We say that from their information ocean they can share with us and learn with us to discover the information they need to know more about themselves, their problems and how they may choose to keep their problems or change themselves. One result of this is that we often understand better the personal maps clients bring to counselling. These maps, as we indicated earlier, are representations of reality and are filtered through sensory representational processes. These representations of reality are further endorsed and encoded through the particular language used by clients and the way they predicate their realities, which they express in and out of the counselling sessions. Reality in this precept is represented from a 'bottom-up' system of sensory–neurolinguistic processes. However in our experience our clients also represent their problems and realities utilizing 'top-down' processes.

Top-down and Bottom-up Counselling: A Two-way Street

In our view NLP counsellors engage in top-down as well as bottom up counselling with clients. Let us be more explicit about what we mean.

When we engage in top-down counselling with clients we create conditions whereby clients can get access to their higher levels of thinking, planning, decision making and control and how they might implement these in their lives. The same may be said of utilizing our clients' abilities to retrieve information they have stored in their memories about events, places and solutions to problems they may have had in the past. We are interested in how they can apply these mentations and memories to resolve their existing problems as they are represented by clients. NLP counselling also involves clients in discovering how these solutions can be transferred from the counselling clinic to the experiences of everyday life. What we might call transferring solutions into new patterns that are ecologically acceptable to clients and others.

Conversely, in bottom-up counselling, which is just as important, we are curious as NLP counsellors to discover with our clients their preferred, habitual or automatic ways of representing their personal realities to themselves. We observed earlier how we do this in visual, auditory, kinaesthetic and olfactory/ gustatory ways so that they form the keystones to the assumed reality of individuals.

Top-down counselling is useful for counsellors in a number of important ways. First of all, it helps them to follow the way clients map their personal realities. Second, it enables them to know better where to 'meet' the client in counselling. By this we mean that, if a client is processing her experiences and is in what we call 'bottom-up mode' then the counsellor adopts a similar approach to this part of the counselling session. Conversely, if someone is engaged in top-down processing such as abstract reasoning, thinking about the meaning of their experiences and how they might decide and plan new ways to experience different situations, the counsellor engages in the top-down mode at these points in counselling.

NLP Counselling and Mental Representatives of Information
●

As you will have gathered by now, in NLP counselling we do not regard clients as being simply passive receptors of stimuli from within themselves or the world around them. We consider the mind of the client to be dynamic and active. In our opinion clients are actively and continuously processing the information they receive from the world around them and from within themselves. But they do much more than this — like ourselves they are busy *transforming* the information they receive into new forms and categories which are registered as a person's experience. Some of these categories will be shared information and others highly idiosyncratic and only relevant to them personally.

Gathering Information from Clients

Because of the abundance of information that clients have at their disposal, no NLP counsellor need ever be stuck, or at a loss in working with clients. Clients who are quiet or silent; who are talkative or noisy; who express their emotions in counselling or who apparently show no emotion at all — all have something in common. They are all revealing some kind of information about themselves.

One of the most crucial tasks for the counsellor using NLP in counselling is to gather information with, for, and about the client. Early in our NLP counselling sessions we like to calibrate the current state of the client, how she is feeling and the lead systems and sensory representations she is using with regard to herself and others. We also believe it is helpful to know what kinds of synaesthesias clients are using as strategies for representing their present map of reality and the problems they say they face and need to resolve.

Sifting, Sorting and Selecting Information

In NLP counselling clients engage in a great deal of sifting, sorting and selecting: of information and personal problems; of the choices they believe they have had available to resolve their problems; and of the kinds of experiences they wish to have and the outcomes these may bring about. And of course clients and counsellors frequently subject to the same process the kinds of information they will or will not work with during counselling sessions and outside the counselling clinic. In NLP counselling the counsellor works with the client to find those strains of information that she wishes to work with and to ignore those aspects of personal information which are not useful to her at present. To do this the client also sorts out the information she brings into counselling which is useful for her to utilize in her efforts to solve her problems or change her personal map of reality. An illustration is provided by the following story.

THE LIBRARIAN AND THE LIBRARY USERS

One day two friends went into their local library to borrow books. The first one spent four hours scanning the shelves. He then left the library frustrated and annoyed that he could not find what he was looking for and had to come away empty-handed. The second person needed only 30 minutes to find what she needed and came away satisfied, with two books. When the friends met later in a café, the woman asked the man why he had failed to find a book that was of interest and why his search had taken so long. The man said he could not be bothered to go through every shelf in the library and he did not know what he was looking for; in any case, finding all of the information in the library was such a difficult task that he had given up. He asked how his friend had been so quick to find two books when she had spent so little time perusing the library shelves. The friend said it was easy — she had consulted the librarian. After a brief discussion the librarian had pointed her in the right direction and the information she wanted was on the shelves right in front of her eyes.

What does this little story tell us about gathering information? First, we have lots of information available to us. Second, we need to know where to look for information that is significant to us. This information is personal. Each client has the need to sort, sift and then select the information appropriate to themselves. The librarian helped the second person to do this. The first person simply hoped they would find something by just going over and looking at the books on the shelves. The librarian created the conditions whereby the library user who consulted him could sort through the books available in the library to see which ones met her particular interests.

NLP counsellors are like the librarian in our story. We help clients to enter the library of their mind. We set out to create the conditions in counselling that allow clients ready access to personal information which they may choose to bring into their counselling sessions in the clinic and to work on in-between counselling sessions. Just as the librarian shows readers how to find printed information, so NLP counsellors afford clients the essential opportunity to sift, sort and select *personal* information. Information is power, and the personal information of clients provides the basis upon which counsellors can empower clients to make new choices and changes in themselves or in perceived problems in their lives. Sometimes the personal information clients require is readily available and is quickly retrieved by them. Sometimes it may be available but require reordering and clarifying before it can be used for change in the personal reality of the client.

There may be occasions when a client has too little or too much information available to them in their counselling sessions. At these times the counsellor should be vigilant and check with the client that the sort of information they need is available to them or that they have not been overwhelmed by too much information or by information of the wrong type.

Insufficient Information

We need information to live sane and normal lives. Without it we become bored, restless, anxious, agitated or angry. Most of the time we have sufficient information to manage to run our lives. Sometimes clients just need sufficient and more appropriate information to make new choices and overcome their problems. Many personal problems can be rectified through obtaining the necessary information.

On the other hand, the most extreme forms of insufficient information can amount to physical, mental and emotional deprivation, and so be highly stressful, depressing and disorienting to clients. In the prolonged absence of information, a state of numbing boredom can progressively envelop the individual. Brian Keenan (1992) poignantly captures the extreme effects of being exposed to prolonged absence of information. In his dark cell, silent as the tomb, deep down in the ground, he recalls:

> I begin as I have always begun these days to think of something, anything upon which I can concentrate. Something I can think about and so try to push away the crushing emptiness of this tiny, tiny cell and the day's long silence. I try with desperation to recall the dream of the night before or perhaps to push away the horror of it. The nights are filled with dreaming. The cinema of the mind, the reels flashing and flashing by and suddenly stopping at some point when some absurd drama I cannot understand ...
>
> Anger overcomes imagination and boredom begins to set in ...
>
> (Keenan, 1992)

When we are deprived of information for long periods of time we suffer. We get bored. We find ways to make up for the absence of the necessary information we need for a stable, satisfying life. In its more extreme form a prolonged absence of information creates a need for stimulation in people. Sometimes this need is so great that we make up new realities. We fantasize, hallucinate, go crazy — anything to compensate for the acute lack of information. A life without information is a life of psychological disturbance that can lead to serious psychiatric illness.

However, in our experience, we find most clients who come to our clinics for NLP counselling sessions have personal problems associated with less pronounced forms of information deprivation. Clients simply do not have enough information upon which to act, to feel and think about or solve their problems. This may be caused by the way clients create a cognitive or sensory representation of their personal problems for themselves or express them to others. At other times clients need only to be nudged in another direction to find the necessary information for that moment and that problem. In our view too much time is wasted on endless pursuits of counsellors' agendas when the client only needs the kind of information that is sufficient for them to deal with a particular part of their life at a particular point and at a particular time with specific people and in identifiable circumstances.

We are reminded of the client who came to counselling saying that she had a lifetime fear of injections. It all started when she had been diagnosed as suffering from diabetes. Part of the problem was that she worked herself up into a highly stressful state prior to each injection and it was not so much the act but the anticipation of puncturing her skin which gave rise to panic by the time she actually administered the insulin to herself. One way of solving this problem with the client would have been to conduct a few sessions of progressive relaxation with systematic desensitization; and this would probably have helped her to manage her 'needle phobia' better . However the NLP counsellor, on finding out what personal information the client had and did not have, suggested that all the client required was sufficient information to counter the anxiety-inducing thoughts which led to her panic about injecting. The following is an excerpt from the final stages of a useful NLP counselling session.

Needle Phobia: A Case of Insufficient Information

COUNSELLOR: So Clara, I wonder what you could say has made a difference to you ... now you feel so much better about injecting yourself ...

CLARA: It's true, I do feel differently about injecting myself ... I don't have that ... panicky feeling ... when I'm doing it ...

COUNSELLOR: Doing it ...

CLARA: Yes, when I'm injecting myself ... but before that as well ... it's really OK now. I seem to have made a lot of fuss ... being silly and worked up about it before.

COUNSELLOR: And now?

CLARA: Now I honestly don't think about it a great deal of the time ... I don't get worked up now ... you know ... worrying before it happens ... not any more ... I just do it ...

COUNSELLOR: *Now* you don't get worked up any more ... is that not interesting? How do you ... do that now?

CLARA: It seems to have happened since I have been coming here to the counselling clinic ... I remember some of what has happened ... I mean, I didn't know how to stop the panics before ...

COUNSELLOR: Before ...

CLARA: Well, not until ... I got the information pack about diabetes ... But more, I suppose, I met some other folk and they seemed to look forward to their injections and seemed proud about the way they were living ... I mean they were coping ... living a full and busy life ... I suppose I began to think about it differently at that point ... I started to think these injections are good for me and ... you know ... saw them as part of my ... routine and ... that's when things changed ...

COUNSELLOR: You seem to be saying something important, Clara ... I wonder what it is ...

CLARA: Er ... I have started, no, I am thinking about it all differently now ... Well, for about six weeks — yes about six weeks ...

COUNSELLOR: And in these six weeks ...

CLARA: I know more now than when I first came for help.

COUNSELLOR: That's right. You now know more than you knew when you first came for help to the clinic ... and now you have more information about yourself and others ... How does that help you now?

CLARA: I know it helps ... I don't know how exactly, but having this new information ... has changed the way I feel ... about injecting my insulin ... I feel a whole lot better and relaxed about the whole thing ...

COUNSELLOR: That is great, Clara ... you now have all the information you need ... and you ... can continue to use your new information to feel better about it all now ... you're relaxed.

Excessive Information

Clients also frequently come to counselling suffering from a state of information overload. There are some typical characteristics of such clients. They often report being confused and in a conflict and generally indecisive about what to do, what to think and what to feel about their personal difficulties. In these cases it is not insufficient information but an excess of information which is at the root of their personal concerns. They have too much information, too many choices, too many thoughts, too many feelings. They have personal information in abundance.

In these cases clients are not simply suffering from a personal pain, grief or anguish, or from disabling distress. Understood within an NLP approach to counselling, their *main* problem is seen to be one of information overload. Quintessentially it is frequently information overload which gives rise to many of the symptomatic problems of stress, fatigue, conflict and emotional turmoil experienced by clients in their personal relationships and private lives. As Alvin Toffler (1971) made clear in his now classic book, *Future Shock*, many people are engulfed by information:

> While some human responses to novelty are involuntary, others are preceded by conscious thought, and this depends upon our ability to absorb, manipulate, evaluate and retain information.
>
> Rational behaviour, in particular, depends upon a ceaseless flow of data from the environment. It depends upon the power of the individual to predict, with at least fair success, the outcome of his/her own actions; to do this, he/she

must be able to predict how the environment will respond to his/her acts. Sanity itself thus hinges on man's ability to predict his/her immediate future on the basis of information fed him/her by the environment ...

In short, the more rapidly changing and novel the environment, the more information the individual needs to process in order to make effective, rational decisions. *Yet just as there are limits on how much sensory input we can accept, there are in-built constraints on our ability to process information.* (Emphasis added)

(Toffler, 1971)

Many of the clients we see for NLP counselling have reached the limits of their ability to process the personal information that is available to them and relevant to their lives. Others are simply flooded by personal information. Paradoxically, in these cases, we regard most clients as having the abilities to resolve their own problems but as being thwarted from doing so by information overload. Ironically it is this very excess of information that clients in counselling have difficulty with in making new choices to change their lives. Sometimes they are confused, sometimes they are in conflict and sometimes they are simply overwhelmed by the rich range of choices they have available to them. The task for the NLP counsellor in these circumstances is to help clients discover and better manage their excessive information. We find that, when our clients can manage their personal information, they can overcome their problems and begin to regain control of their lives.

Case Example of Excessive Information

Eric, a 29-year-old computer programmer, came to the clinic for counselling about his private life and problems relating to women at work. Eric talked fluently and rapidly. There was no stopping him. The counsellor encouraged Eric to keep talking. The result was that there was no control in the counselling session. There was just too much information to deal with. The counsellor noticed that Eric skipped from topic to topic. One moment he would be talking about his childhood and then suddenly he would make an association with something he had read in a magazine, heard on the radio or seen on television. At these times he would sometimes say, "That is what is wrong with me — do you think it is hereditary?"

Eric moved so swiftly from one situation to the next that he never spent enough time on the one thing he needed to do most — limit and order the amount of information he was trying to manage. When he could do that, he would begin to focus on examining his concerns and problems he was experiencing in his life. It soon became clear that Eric lived much of his life the way he approached his job. He gathered information; he specialized in the pursuit of information; he was an expert on information. And he suffered the consequences.

The NLP counsellor decided that Eric's job as a computer programmer could be a useful metaphor to use in his counselling sessions, so he worked with Eric using the metaphor of programming information as a way of enabling him to limit the amount of information he was handling, to sort out and order relevant information and to separate the signals that really mattered to him from the noise of everyday life. Eric started to make progress. From this point on, his counselling sessions consisted of tidying up his personal programmes and carrying out tasks set by the counsellor. The more in charge of 'programming' he became, the more he came to regain control over his life. One other outcome of this work with Eric was that changes began to occur in his perceptions, attitudes and behaviour towards women and work.

NLP Counselling with Hot and Cold Information
●

The counsellor also needs to be aware of the presence of hot and cold information and its influence on clients and the way they experience their reality of everyday life, or specific situations which may be concerning them. Richard Lazarus, the leading psychologist, showed in his studies of stress and coping how people use two types of information in their efforts to adapt to the demands made on them in their lives. Hot and cold information deserve a special mention in NLP counselling. Hot information is information about feelings. Cold information is about facts. In NLP counselling we find that, fundamentally, clients are engaged in processing these two types of information. As counsellors using NLP with clients we need to know three things about our work with the personal information of clients: (1) we need to be aware when the client is using hot or cold information; (2) we need to know how to pace and lead the client in her search for new choices based on the information she has available to her and the kinds of new personal information she may need in order to make changes in her life and her individual map of reality; (3) we need to be able to formulate appropriate counselling questions that will enable clients to make this possible as part of their personal process of change (see Table 7).

It is important for us to notice that hot information is present when the client is talking about their feelings or expressing them in a direct way such as breaking down and crying in the counselling session whenever they talk about a particular aspect of a personal problem. Cold information is present when the client is processing information by providing recalled facts or figures or specific data about an event, place, person or experience.

When clients are talking about their feelings they are in the observing mode of functioning. Hot information can be talked about without due discomfort or obvious distress. For instance, a client talked about how angry she used to get when her husband gambled her savings and came home drunk after gambling at the weekends. This is hot information, but in the observing mode. Hot information in the *experiencing* mode is more direct in its expression. Another client who had been diagnosed as suffering from post-traumatic stress disorder said she was still hurting inside. As she said it she spontaneously burst into tears and re-experienced some of the events leading up to a plane crash which she had survived, along with three other people.

Counsellors need to be able to make it possible for clients to move from the observing mode of talking about hot information into the experiencing mode. There is a saying in NLP counselling that captures this sense of directly experiencing our feelings: 'clients need to feel the heat of their own feelings'. Equally

Table 7: Counselling with hot and cold information: useful questions for clients	
Hot information: **processing emotions/feelings**	**Cold information:** **processing facts/data**
I wonder how that feels?	When did you feel that way?
What are you feeling now?	Who makes you feel that way?
Could you just feel that feeling ?	Where does it happen?
What feelings did these thoughts give you in the past?	When you look back, what do you think started it all?
What feelings do these thoughts give you now?	What do you think has changed?
Can you help me understand the emotions you are experiencing at such times?	When specifically did these changes take place?
	Who was involved?
How would I/he/she/they know what you are feeling now?	How long have you had this problem?
Where is this feeling located in you?	What has to happen for this problem to be resolved?
If you asked that feeling to show itself, what would it be like/how would it express itself to you now?	How do you stop it from happening?
	When/where/with whom/ does it not happen?
What would you like to feel instead?	How will you know when this problem has been solved?

counsellors using NLP counselling should be aware of when the client is in the cold information mode of processing information and when this is *useful* for the purposes of counselling and when it is not. For example, there is little point in continuing counselling session after counselling session in the cold information mode when a person needs to experience their feelings about a particular set of circumstances they are relating to their counsellor. Similarly someone who continuously uses the counselling session to cry without identifying the source of the crying or what they would like to do about it in the future is stuck. In circumstances like these, it is often the NLP counsellor's task to help the client to reclaim control of their feelings.

Disorganizing and Reorganizing Personal Information

●

Clearly we can see how personal information is central to NLP counselling. NLP counsellors help clients to sift, sort and select the kind of information they need to work on in counselling sessions and the information they need to obtain to bring into counselling sessions where the clear purpose of the session is working with hot and cold information. Sometimes clients will not need to be led into resolving their problems. Many clients simply need enough rapport, trust, respect and understanding and a 'space' within which they can reorder their lives and make the choices necessary and significant to them. This can be enough to bring about change. The change may be small, but important — not all changes need to be of mammoth proportions for clients to benefit from NLP counselling. Indeed it is sometimes only a small change or new choice that a client makes that is sufficient for them to be satisfied, so that no further counselling is required.

For instance, in our experience only a few NLP counselling sessions are required for clients who want to overcome a great range of phobias and situations in which they become unreasonably anxious. Similarly clients who need to enhance their self-confidence, to break undesirable habits such as nail-biting or to reduce tension headaches obtain relief with brief NLP counselling. They often have the personal information which the NLP counsellor can utilize within the counselling session whereby they can set up the changes they wish to make to the pattern of their behaviour. Other clients experiencing stress as a result of more entrenched personal difficulties, such as those of their sexual identity, rape, addictions, physical abuse and damaging personal relationships, may need many more counselling sessions before new possibilities are considered and changes can be made to their personal maps of reality.

Success in NLP counselling can be defined as the client achieving a personal outcome in a desired state different from the outcomes and state they are experiencing at present. Although different in many respects, short-term and long-term NLP counselling, when successful, have one thing in common: they create a safe therapeutic environment within which new choices and personal changes can be made by clients in counselling. This means going through a process with each client where they move from a state of disorganizing their personal information to reorganizing it in such a way that they can obtain more satisfying outcomes in their lives.

When clients are organized they can predict and control their choices in life. For those choices that are outside their control they are able to reorganize their personal information sufficiently to accept those things they cannot change or to find other choices that are within their control. The task for the NLP counsellor is to assist clients in their desire to move away from their present state of disorganizing into a different and desired state: a new direction, a reorganizing of themselves. It is then that change takes place.

Chapter 7

THE 'MAGICAL' LANGUAGE OF METAPHOR

Metaphor and Language in Human Experience

●

In NLP counselling we find it is helpful to construe metaphor as 'a universal way of using terms, or making references to, or for one or many things; to describe another or others because of some similarity between them or between their relations'. Lakoff and Johnson in their marvellous book, *Metaphors We Live By*, define a metaphor as 'understanding and experiencing one kind of thing in terms of another'. Let us explain more fully what we mean.

When we describe the colour blue we are not describing the actual experience of the colour we describe as blue, but are using the word to get near what we are experiencing. Maybe we refine it somewhat and say it is light blue, which gets closer to our experience. Perhaps we try further and say it is an azure blue or a milky blue. But as counsellors we notice that what has happened is that we have had to change something to describe our experience. We have introduced adjectives to make more sense of the noun which represents our experience. In a similar way, when a client describes herself as feeling 'blue', we do not think of actual colours but we share or assume some of the feeling captured in the metaphor of language: we infer that they are talking about their feelings. The way clients speak and use language to describe their feelings in this way is usually confirmed by them when they go on to say they are sad, low or tearful, or that they cannot sleep very well and wake up early in the morning.

This is just one example of the way we use metaphor to communicate our experiences to others and try to make sense of them for ourselves. Metaphor is thus not literal and can have many connotations for clients in counselling as well as for the counsellors who provide counselling.

In NLP counselling, language is a metaphor for experience. A word of caution here: although we may share the same language and therefore have a basis for understanding our clients, this is no guarantee that we will always understand them. For instance, many people just use the one word 'snow' to describe the frozen flakes that fall from the sky. But experienced skiers use the lexicon of 'snow' as a metaphor to further refine what they mean when they are talking about snow to other skiers. They say the snow is fine as powder or crunchy as corn. Furthermore it has been reported that eskimos may have as many as 23 different words they use to describe their experiences of what we evoke with the one word, 'snow'. One word or phrase can be a metaphor to describe one or many experiences and many words can be used to describe one single experience.

The NLP counsellor must be aware of the many ways clients use language as a metaphor to describe their experiences and what they see as personal problems. In many instances we may infer that the client who says she is feeling 'blue' is experiencing sadness or even perhaps some sort of state of depression. However it is perfectly feasible for a person experiencing difficulties to mean something entirely different, yet use the same language. It is therefore imperative that the NLP counsellor does not make presumptions simply because of what the client says. Language is only a metaphor for the client's experience: it is not *what* the client experiences. Robert James Waller describes Joe in *The Bridges of Madison County*:

He liked words and images. 'Blue' was one of his favourite words. He liked the feeling it made on his lips and tongue when he said it. Words have physical feeling, not just meaning, he remembered thinking when he was young. He liked other words, such as 'distant', 'woodsmoke', 'highway', 'ancient', 'passage', 'voyager' and 'India'. Joe loved how they sounded, how they tasted and what they conjured up in his mind.

(Waller, 1993)

In NLP counselling language is used in an attempt to relate to the experience the client calls a problem. Language is an essential prerequisite, without which we would not get near understanding clients, but it is a metaphor, a doorway which we may approach, stand at, and walk through, with or without our clients, in our efforts at helping.

Language as a metaphor of human experience fits comfortably within NLP counselling and some of the assumptions we hold about the way people create the experiences they have at any time or place or within any given moment. The clients' use of language in counselling is similar in a very important way to their use of sensory representational systems. They use language to create their personal reality. In NLP counselling language is conceptualized as a representational system. It is verbal and non-verbal in content and structure and it is concerned with personal meaning and experience. To this extent, language is a metaphor used by all clients and counsellors in their counselling sessions, a key that can unlock what the client is experiencing and how she uses language to communicate her thinking and feelings arising from the personal mental maps and the perceived problems she brings to counselling.

Case Example One: 'Feeling Blue'

A 48-year-old man called Danny, who came for counselling, described himself as 'feeling blue'. He was in the process of becoming divorced and made redundant — reason enough, you might think, for anyone to be upset or at least sad. Some counsellors might not be blamed for assuming that in these circumstances the man was somewhat depressed, an assumption apparently confirmed when he described himself as feeling blue.

But on gathering information that was relevant to him, Danny said it was being blue that worried him more than anything else. It turned out that being blue was the root of his problems. For him, 'being blue' meant that his marriage had not gone right since his heart condition; it meant being cold and distant towards his wife and friends; it meant he could not take the risk of going for job promotions. He believed being blue would stop him from getting another job. And for him being blue was the reason he was being made redundant.

Being blue did not just mean being sad or depressed to Danny, as the counsellor discovered: blue was the colour of his face and lips when his heart was not working properly; being blue was a circulation problem and the fear of having one of his legs amputated. These were *his* concerns. This is what 'being blue' meant to *him*.

The course of NLP counselling in this case then took a radically different turn. When the counsellor asked Danny if he knew what colour he would like to be, Danny said, with considerable alacrity, "Pink. I want to be pink. I want to be healthy. Pink lips, pink legs, healthy heart and a nice face again."

Human experience is full of personal metaphors: some we share and understand; some we do not share; some we think we share but do not understand. Language is a metaphor we all use in our efforts to describe and explain ourselves, our situations, our pains, problems, worries, happiness, sorrows and successes. Metaphors can also be non-verbal: body posture and movements, the position of hands, feet, arms, legs and head, and facial display and expression are all examples of metaphors.

Therefore, it is our understanding that metaphors are the means by which we try to be understood and to understand ourselves and the world around us. It follows that metaphors can also be symbolized internally or externally and codified by each one of us to give meaning to the world of our experience. At the same time, the way we use these metaphors to represent our reality makes up what we call individual experience. Metaphors are our way of synthesizing our sensory representations and codifying them in the language we use and the beliefs we have about ourselves and other people and the situations within which we find ourselves. Our metaphors are the way we understand our world. They constitute what we say we understand and do not understand as well as our attempts at understanding our personal, social and cultural life. In NLP counselling we utilize metaphor in a very broad, encompassing way that allows us to help clients by accommodating many ideas, understandings and experiences. The way we are using metaphor here then assumes the inclusion of literal description, perceived description and similes, analogies, stories, songs, poetry, anecdotes, homonyms, homographs and homophones and other artful and linguistic forms.

NLP Counselling: A Metaphor for Helping Clients

●

Clearly language — verbal and non-verbal — plays a large part in what we do in NLP counselling. It is one way of creating the conditions for change in clients' lives. We talk; we set tasks; we work with clients to discover the outcomes they want to experience that are different from those they are currently experiencing and how these might be brought about. NLP counselling is thus a metaphor for helping — just one way of deciding how we might help people change, should they wish to do so. Its effectiveness can be measured in discussions with other counsellors and colleagues, and by conducting research into its processes and outcomes. Counsellors will also provide some of their own answers, but the acid test is the way clients tell their stories in counselling: the language they use and the way they represent their personal realities to the counsellor.

Sources of Metaphor

●

Stories, anecdotes, folktales and fables all provide the counsellor with a rich source of metaphor. Poems, songs and paintings can be introduced into counselling when this seems appropriate and fits well with the situation or experience a client is struggling to resolve. Dance and mime are also available to the counsellor who finds this mode of presenting metaphors in counselling potentially useful and interesting to clients in the resolution of their personal difficulties.

Yet the vast potential of metaphor in counselling has often been overlooked by counsellors. Distinguished writers and therapists such as Bruno Bettleheim have shown how metaphors can be an enchanting experience for people who want to resolve personal problems. And David Gordon (1978) writes:

> Explicit metaphors are also useful as a way of aiding a client in seeking and considering new choices for himself within the context of the 'problem'. These metaphors typically occur as anecdotes or full-blown stories which are either 'true' or are tailored to suit the client's situation. Such metaphors can act as tremendously effective agents of change, particularly when they are constructed and implemented according to the models of metaphor building.
>
> (Gordon, 1978)

Client Metaphors

●

Clients bring a rich range of metaphors to their counselling sessions. Often it is their use of metaphor which makes the counselling process helpful to them — provided that the counsellor is alert to what is going on. We have seen how a client's use of language is an approximation of her experience, but clients also use language in more symbolic and analogical ways, along with their body movements and even their feelings, to express metaphorically their experience at any one time.

When clients use metaphors in NLP counselling they can come thick, quick and furious. They can be brought into counselling in their droves of diversity or they can come in one at a time, with a single theme. One client who received counselling over a number of sessions and changed as a result said very little to begin with, before making small but personally significant changes in her life.

Case Example Two: Making a Mark in Life

Jan, a 37-year-old, timid woman, an only child of domineering and ageing parents, came to counselling and sat for her first session saying very little and clutching a thick book. She said over and over again, "This is my book, this is my book, it's my book, my stamps, my book, my stamps." The counsellor acknowledged this and Jan again said it was her book of stamps. She then spent three more sessions going into great detail about her stamps and the positions they must have in the book and how they should be presented and the precise stories that went along with each one. Each stamp had to be stuck down firmly, but not so firmly that it would be stuck down forever, just in case she needed to put it in another place. She made a particular point of emphasizing how there were individual markings on each stamp and how they were all different although to a casual observer they might look the same. As counselling progressed, other things were happening, but the main theme was the stamps and Jan stuck to this theme through each session. After some time the counsellor began to understand that the stamps were a metaphor for Jan and the way she was trying to gain some recognition and control over her life.

When she realized that the counsellor accepted what she was saying, and took a genuine interest and tried to help her, Jan wanted to talk more and more about her stamps — and a good job it was too, as this was the turning point for this client. The stamps, Jan discovered, were her way of making her mark in life. The stamps were her metaphor: her way of telling her story, of attempting to understand her present experience. Jan had nearly always done what her parents had told her to do, against her better judgement. She recalled how in the past she had been called a 'bad girl' by her parents, who said that they would have to do something about all her screaming and shouting and stamping about. They frequently said to her something that made her feel guilty, angry and helpless. "You don't care about us; you can stamp around, but you will never make your mark in life." When she recalled these events Jan was flooded by tears and anger, followed by a stream of relief at releasing these strong emotions. She then started to talk about the many things in life that she felt she had missed and that she now wanted to experience.

*Case Example Three: Kicking Feet**

There is a story that illustrates the power of understanding and using metaphor in counselling. It is about a woman who came to counselling because of her kicking feet. Helena had considerable difficulty getting a good night's sleep. Each night shortly after falling asleep she would be woken by her feet and legs going into a muscular spasm and making violent kicking movements.

Rapport was created by the NLP counsellor, personal information was gathered and she was checked for night cramps or tremor. None existed. It was discovered that Helena had had this problem for 12 years, ever since she was discriminated against because of her age and badly treated by her boss. After working slavishly and loyally for him for many years, she was given paltry wages and told to take a junior job because a younger person would be taking over from her. She was told she would have a little place in the corner of the room and the new person would have her desk and office. As in the past, she did exactly what her boss told her to do, without any complaint. She went into the corner of the office without saying how upset and angry she was at the way she had been treated, but this was Helena's way of trying to deal with the situation the way she knew best.

She went home and never spoke to anyone about her ordeal; those few people who knew about it never brought it up in conversation as it was a 'taboo' subject. For the first few months Helena was restless and agitated and never went out. After a while she found she could get off to sleep at night, but she would soon wake up with a start. A curious thing began to happen. Her feet and legs started going into spasm. Each night they would start kicking and kept on kicking, for no apparent reason. This went on all those years before Helena sought help from a counsellor who used metaphor in his work with clients.

Initially rapport was developed with Helena. The counsellor asked her to tell her story, which she had hidden away all that time. During counselling Helena at first kept her feet quite still and she sat erect, just as a secretary might have done when she was sitting at her desk. The counsellor adopted a similar position. As the sessions progressed he increasingly matched her body

---

* I am grateful to Stephen Brooks, who first told me this story. I have adapted it with minor changes to emphasize the importance of using metaphor in NLP counselling.

posture and breathing and in particular the positions of Helena's legs and feet. She had got to the point in her story where she said she did not know what she felt about her boss now or if her 'kicking feet' would ever stop.

At this point the counsellor asked Helena if she ever wondered what her feet were trying to tell her. He said that, if she did not object, he would talk to her feet, as they were kicking for a very good reason. Helena looked slightly confused but was comfortable and in a trusting state of rapport and readily agreed that this seemed a very good idea. The counsellor started to talk to Helena's feet: "Feet, you have been trying to tell Helena something for some time. You do this at night. When she has just dropped off to sleep you start kicking. I would like you to feel free to start kicking any time in the next few minutes. You could do little kicks or big kicks as she sits in the chair or as she wonders which foot might kick first."

After a few moments, Helena's feet began to make little movements and the counsellor commented that this was very interesting; he said that maybe that night Helena would discover something in her dreams, as she woke up or as she went to sleep. At the next counselling session, when Helena came in, she looked straight into the counsellor's eyes. She was different. Relieved, alert and excited, she began to tell the counsellor that something wonderful had happened the night after her counselling session and as a result of it she had resigned from her job and 'told her boss off' for treating her so badly all those years. The counsellor wondered about the kicking feet. Helena said in a relaxed and composed voice that it was the 'oddest thing'. She seemed to be free from the kicking for the first time in years.

The counsellor had accepted Helena's kicking as a metaphor about her experience. He did not know what the kicking meant. Neither did Helena. But she soon found out. When she was able to kick her boss out of her life and leave him behind, she was free to choose a fresh future. It was at this point that she ceased to suffer from her kicking feet.

Case Example Four: Tony and the Tennis Shoes

Tony, a skinny, timid 15-year-old boy came with his mother for his first counselling session about his 'anorexia nervosa'. The counsellor created rapport with Tony and his mother and then started to ask Tony questions about his eating behaviour. But his mother answered every question put to Tony. This was consistent with the reports of other caring and health professionals: the mother was seen as a domineering woman who ran Tony's life for him. She had taken Tony to see dieticians, nurses and psychiatrists before she brought him to the NLP counselling clinic. He had had behaviour therapy and medication; diets and emergency nursing care; rewards for 'correct behaviour'; and highly structured and routine feeding schedules — all set up for him by his mother and others. Tony did not speak much to begin with at the counselling session.

The history of Tony's birth showed that he had had the umbilical cord wrapped around his neck. A current theory about his eating behaviour was that having the cord around his neck had traumatized Tony and he had repressed his memory of choking. It seemed plausible and might even have been right. After all, Tony only ate yogurts and had to have all of the food that he did eat on occasions put through the liquidizer. Some of this theory also fitted the idea that Tony was being kept at the baby stage by his mother: she could handle him as a baby but not as a teenager. There may have been some logic to this view, which may have been true or false. What it did not explain was the fact that for three years Tony seemed to eat very well indeed: solid foods, meat and vegetables, fruit and fibre, and junk food.

Several questions confronted the counsellor. Should the birth trauma theory be pursued? Would it be better to work with the mother? She seemed to be dominant in the relationship with her son. Could change only come with her support and commitment to a further eating programme for Tony? Should Tony be seen on his own for counselling and building up his confidence to challenge his mother? Maybe he would start eating more and different food. Maybe not.

During a counselling session the counsellor did notice *one* time when Tony spoke clearly and confidently about himself. It was about his tennis shoes. Tony was wearing a pair of professional tennis shoes. Real tennis shoes — not trainers, expensive tennis shoes — the ones worn by top players and seen on television in national tournaments. Tony's mother did not know much about tennis but she was willing to help him all she could to get into tennis, but only if he would start eating first. After this the counsellor only spoke to Tony. He started talking back to the counsellor and his mother stopped answering for Tony because she did not have the knowledge to take part in the conversation. The counsellor said to Tony: "Tell me all you know about tennis, because your shoes are saying to me 'Tony knows about tennis', and I want to listen to you telling me about tennis."

Tony surprised everybody in the counselling session that day. He talked about particular tennis stars, the shoes and shirts they wore and the training they did. He went into great detail about different tennis matches and how each player had won or prepared for the game. He said that he really wanted to be a tennis player and some day wanted a coach to improve his game. He was already senior school champion. Here was a side of Tony that no one had seen or heard about before. When conversation focused on his 'anorexia nervosa' he was subdued and fiddled around, looking uninterested in the exchanges taking place between his mother and doctors, nurses and psychiatrists. But he could talk tennis all day long. He was animated, alert, confident, and felt good about himself when he talked tennis. Tennis was a significant metaphor for Tony and he was motivated and positive and became enlivened when he talked about it.

As the counselling session progressed the NLP counsellor used the metaphor of tennis and tennis shoes to talk more with Tony. He said how on listening to Tony he knew he was an expert on tennis. He said that he really believed Tony was seriously interested in becoming a tennis player and that everybody knew that tennis players had to prepare for their game. They had to have the right shoes and shirts and they had to pace themselves. Tennis was a game where you just absorbed the way great tennis players played. Studying their preparation and putting it into practice was also essential to becoming a great tennis player. Tennis players had a great deal of energy and an appetite for every match. Because Tony was 15, the NLP counsellor said, "Every star in the game started preparing early in their lives, some when they were

14 or 15, or before their next birthday." Tony was asked if there was one player he could study and learn from. He could think about it, or make a choice as he was going home or before he left the counselling clinic. The session continued in this way with the theme of counselling acting as a metaphor that spoke to Tony and not his mother, so that Tony could speak for himself.

Towards the end of the session the counsellor was still talking to Tony and listening to what he had to say, to the exclusion of his mother. "Tony," he said, but turning to Tony's mother as he did so, "you know so much about tennis and I have learned a lot from you today. I have one other thing I would like to ask you about tennis. You have said you had an OK coach but wanted to have a better coach one day. What makes an OK coach a better coach?" Tony paused for some time and it seemed that he would not say anything. But he did answer and emphatically. "An OK coach is someone who is always with you and tries to help you — but they get it wrong a lot of times."

"That's right, Tony, they get in the way of the player developing his own abilities, skills and confidence. A good coach knows when to step out of the way and let the player do it their way." As the counsellor said this to Tony, he glanced over at his mother and then said, "Did you hear that? A good coach lets you do it the best way you know how. A good coach knows when to keep their mouth shut."

In conclusion he said: "Tennis players play better tennis when they can prepare in the way you have described to us today. Thanks, Tony. I do like your shoes they are a real tennis player's shoes — you can tell. You know what you are talking about."

Only seven days after this counselling session, Tony's mother rang the clinic to say that Tony had started eating 'normally' again. She was amazed at the changes that had taken place in his eating behaviour. She could not understand why he had stopped eating solid foods or why he had started again. He now had a healthy appetite once more.

The Counsellor's Use of Metaphor in Counselling

●

The cases cited show just some of the many ways metaphor can be used in counselling clients. We can use metaphor to create and enhance rapport. Metaphor can often be introduced into the way the NLP counsellor gathers relevant personal information with clients. Metaphor is also used by counsellors to create the conditions whereby clients can make new choices and changes in their lives. The NLP counsellor considers the appropriate use of metaphor as a way of enabling clients to move out of their present state into new and desired states. Put succinctly, the NLP counsellor's sensitive use of metaphor makes it possible for clients to experience the states they say they desire.

As we have seen, counselling can fail if rapport is not created and maintained. However, counselling sometimes makes little progress for other reasons. The counsellor's failure to recognize a metaphoric pattern of communication used by the client and to respond in an appropriate metaphoric manner is one of them. Here is a short extract from a counselling session with a young woman who could swim, and wanted to, but had a fear of swimming in a public swimming pool.

COUNSELLOR: Marlene, how would you describe your fear of swimming in a public swimming pool?

MARLENE: Well, it is like a wall with tubes, that starts closing in on me and I start to feel smaller. Each time I can see me beginning to drown, going down into this wall ... then it turns into a big hole and I am slipping down inside it and I hear people screaming in it. The people screaming at me ... The water is like a giant hand pulling me down under ... it's horrible.

COUNSELLOR: Where does this happen exactly — at the shallow end or the deep end or the middle of the pool?

MARLENE: It can happen anywhere ... any time ... any depth. It draws me in, sucking me down in a swirling feeling ... like a helter-skelter. I start to get dizzy and get panicky ... The hole

... the blackness ... I just know I am going to faint and drown ... in the water ...

COUNSELLOR: You know that is not exactly true, Marlene. You can swim. You can swim at the pool when no one is there, or at your friend's swimming pool when there are just the two of you, so there are times when you do not feel panicky. Am I right?

MARLENE: Yes, but that does not help me. I want to be able to swim with all my friends and go to the local pool and meet other people ... I still panic when I see them looking at me ... anybody looking at me makes me panic.

The counsellor did reasonably well here, but could have made much more progress in this counselling session by using metaphor. Why is this? First of all, Marlene is *using* metaphor in her language. She is describing how she feels and her fear of swimming in a public swimming pool. Second, Marlene is showing that the metaphor she has chosen to describe her problem and experience of fear is *significant* to her. Third, there is a *structure* to the metaphor she is using. Fourth, it *relates* to her concern, for which she is seeking some sort of *resolution* to the problem she describes. Fifth, Marlene is providing the NLP counsellor with a marvellous opportunity to enlarge and develop the *thoroughness* of the metaphor in a way that can be therapeutically useful.

Creating Meaningful Metaphors

Since there are so many metaphors to choose from, how does the counsellor select and construct metaphors that are therapeutic and beneficial and personally significant to clients? We find that when metaphors are therapeutic in counselling our clients are able to match indirectly their personal maps and meanings with the events they are experiencing in their lives. Counsellors therefore need to know how to construct powerful metaphors that pace the present state of clients and create options whereby they can experience desired states in the future. Any metaphor that is not regarded as significant in some way to clients is unlikely to be helpful in creating therapeutic change.

Calibrating Client Metaphors

The NLP counsellor has to calibrate from the client the structure, style and kind of metaphor that can be constructed for therapeutic change to take place. It may come as a surprise to some counsellors, but we have found that the context of a therapeutic metaphor is secondary, if not irrelevant, to therapeutic change. What is essential is that the metaphor used in counselling satisfies the present state needs of the client. In this sense the content of a therapeutic metaphor is simply the surface structure upon which the deeper meaning of the metaphor is experienced by the client; there is a surface structure and a deep structure to the use of metaphor in NLP counselling.

Rather as an artist uses a canvas and paint to create a painting, the NLP counsellor structures a metaphor. It is the meaning of the painting that is significant and not the picture itself. For some a Monet, such as 'The Field of Poppies', will be experienced as simply pretty, while for others it will be a symbol of the power of nature and sexual and primordial energy. For others again the painting will mean nothing more or less than a dull and boring event: they are unmoved by the painting. As a painting is a metaphor that means different things to different people, so the therapeutic metaphor can mean different things to different clients.

This is why the NLP counsellor, as well as being creative, needs some systematic way in which to construct meaningful metaphors tailored to clients in counselling. As the eminent psychiatrist and thinker, Carl Gustav Jung, observed many years ago, 'The least of things with a meaning is worth more in life than the greatest of things without it.' In our own work we have found that it is possible to create useful client metaphors using a seven-point strategy.

Therapeutic metaphors do not just happen by accident. The more we can approximate the structure of the cognitive maps clients may use in counselling, the more likely we can build therapeutic metaphors that can be useful to create changes desired by clients. One effective and efficient way that this can be done is to have an explicit strategy for structuring and building client-based metaphors. Carl Rogers often referred to the importance and validity of the person in client-centred counselling. Our model of creating client-centred metaphors in NLP counselling is similar in some ways.

A therapeutic metaphor should be personally significant to each client and be isomorphic — equal in characteristics — with the context of their problems. It should have a content and be built having regard to the person and their past, present or future concerns and the resolution of a problem they may be experiencing. Moreover to be therapeutic a metaphor must be sufficiently thorough to include or exclude the difficulties the client is facing or wanting to change. We call this the 'relatedness' part of a therapeutic metaphor. Above all, in building therapeutic metaphors we need to take account of the sensory and linguistic processes that each client utilizes to represent and generate their situation or 'problem'. These NLP processes provide us with the personal information upon which we can create therapeutic metaphors with clients in counselling.

The NLP counsellor therefore needs to be satisfied that he knows what makes the metaphor therapeutic for any particular client. The seven-point strategy shown in Table 8 allows us to create a relevant therapeutic metaphor for each client or group of clients. It also makes it possible to construct therapeutic metaphors that are efficient and effective. A therapeutic metaphor is *efficient* when its structure encompasses the main elements of the situations clients face. We can also say that a therapeutic metaphor is *effective* when it provides a way for clients to change from their present state to a more desired state. Finally, a therapeutic metaphor does not have to include *all* of the seven points. It just needs to be sufficiently thorough for it to be a 'good enough' metaphor.

Case Example Five: Jenny and the Children

Jenny was 42, divorced and had two children, Kenny (6) and Davina (8). They lived in perpetual fear of Jenny's ex-husband, Nick, who would come round to their small two-bedroomed end-of-terrace house at any time of day or night and start shouting and swearing and verbally abusing the children and Jenny. Nick would frequently get into a drunken rage and berate his wife and insult her in front of the neighbours. He made unfounded allegations about Jenny sleeping with other men and having affairs with other men in the street where she lived. At other times he was very remorseful and

Table 8: A seven-point strategy for building therapeutic metaphors	
1 Structure	Include in the metaphor a structure analogous to the cognitive or personal maps of the person or persons involved and their positions within a given context.
2 Sensory representation	Calibrate and utilize the sensory representations of clients. If, for example, a client is using a mixture of visual and auditory representations the counsellor builds these into the metaphor for the client. Alternatively, if the client has an obvious and preferred sensory representational system, such as the visual modality, we would emphasize this by building vivid visual elements into the metaphor.
3 Predicates and sub-modalities	Utilize the predicates and sub-modalities in the language of the metaphor in such a way that the person or persons can readily retrieve them and that it reflects their own sensory processes and linguistic activity.
4 Significance	In creating a metaphor, provide a *content* which is significant to the person or persons in such a way that the metaphor is isomorphic — equal in characteristics — to the *context* in which the person or persons experience their problem.
5 Relatedness	The metaphor used should include the main character or characters or things, people or places, time and how they relate to each other in a specific context.

Table 8: A seven-point strategy for building therapeutic metaphors (continued)	
6 Thoroughness	A metaphor is more likely to be therapeutic when it is constructed thoroughly and has been assessed for the range of those persons or things which should be included and deleted and the scope of its purpose.
7 Resolution	To be therapeutic a metaphor should be deliberately created so as to include isomorphically a way or ways whereby a resolution and different outcomes can be found to a problem or problems being experienced by a person or persons.

apologetic and he was equally loud and bellowing in his self-pity.

Several times he had waited outside the house to try and catch Jenny and the children and stop them getting into their home. At other times he would wait outside the house and stop them getting out. At these times, Jenny and the children were prisoners in their own home. They were anxious and fearful. They wanted to feel safe. They wanted a way out.

The seven-point strategy was used to build a therapeutic metaphor that could be introduced during the course of counselling with Jenny and her children. Consider how it was done and think of the many alternative ways you can design therapeutic metaphors for use in counselling clients.

The NLP counsellor decided to build a therapeutic metaphor around the theme that Nick was a worthless, noisy and foul-mouthed troll, a monster that terrorized the queen and frightened the prince and princess who lived in a little, comforting castle. This is how the metaphor was structured and designed:

Table 9: A seven-point strategy case example	
Gathering information	**Metaphor transformation structure**
Jenny/Kenny/Davina	Queen/Prince/Princess
Nick	Troll
seeing Nick roaming around house/shouting abuse, screaming at Jenny/threatening the children	**Sensory representations** visual/auditory and kinaesthetic actions
seeing Nick drunk/using foul language and expressing insulting behaviour	**Predicates and submodalities** the *sight* and *sound* of the Troll and his drunken rocking and rolling *movements*/agressive behaviour as he roars out and shouts abuse
Jenny/Kenny/Davina imprisoned in own house fearful/threat to safety Jenny/Kenny/Davina in conflict with Nick and in fear of him and no freedom to go out of their house	**Significance** inside castle with big strong walls outside, superlock doors inside, safe from the ranting Troll Queen/Prince and Princess in conflict with Troll and in fear of it and trapped in the castle
Profile Jenny/Kenny/Davina fear of Nick/unable to go out of house without fear of Nick/foul language or drunkenness	**Thoroughness** Queen/Prince/Princess safe from the ranting Troll in their castle and its rolling/swaying/ shouting and anger/no effect on them any more
Information Jenny/Kenny/Davina are able to come and go in their house without any fear of Nick and his bouts of drunkenness and abuse and are able to ignore his threats	**Metaphor** Queen/Prince/Princess feel completely safe in their castle as they see the stupefied Troll and hear its rantings as pathetic grunts and ravings but it has no affect on them. A wise wizard who lives in their castle becomes their friend and shares with them a secret way of dealing with dopey Trolls

After a free play session with Kenny and Davina in which Jenny played alongside her children the counsellor said: "That was fun. Isn't it good to remember that life can be what you want it to be as you master the little monsters you fear in life? And as I am saying this you might like to get really comfortable and relaxed and together and just find a space in the playroom so you can be comfortable and rest — a place that is safe for you and you can call your own [he waits until everyone is in the place that they have chosen]. That's right. And now you have found your place that is safe and you can call your very own, you can choose to close your eyes or keep them open, so long as you listen to this story.

"You know there once was a queen and a prince and a princess who all lived in a castle just right for them, and they had doors on the castle that were strong and the castle sparkled in many wonderful and different colours on the inside. And the walls of the castle were so firm that they stood out like a rock on the outside. The queen had a bedroom and the princess and the prince shared a bedroom and the bedrooms were within easy reach of each other and the queen could call to the prince or the princess and they would easily hear her and know to come running and be safe just at the sound of her voice. And do you know what? The prince and the princess could do the same thing — they could call from anywhere in the castle or just outside it and the queen would hear them and know when to be there so everyone could be safe. And it was a very good thing too. They could be safe at any time they chose to be safe within the castle or in their rooms or even outside the castle because they could hear each other and be strong and feel good as they knew they were safe.

"One day a big, noisy and drunken troll came near their castle and as he walked close by he had this rocking and rolling movement and his whole body swayed back and forward like a candle wavering in the wind. He shouted and screamed at the queen and the prince and the princess and used dirty troll words at them. But do you know what happened next? [Pause for Jenny, Kenny and Davina to nod or shake their heads or just to make sure that they are paying attention to the story.] That's right. The queen, the prince and the princess remembered that they could be safe and strong in their castle and the sound of calling each other was stronger than the shouting and cursing of the troll. And just to prove it, you know you can feel safe because everyone knows that a troll says silly things and shouts and does nothing but get drunk and just makes lot of noise. But just to be sure that *you* can do the right thing, the queen and the prince and the princess had a secret passage in and out of the house ... they would always be safe as long as they knew they could call on each other when they needed to, and the other times they could play. And as they found out they could take control of their fear, the troll just sounded boring and his shouting did not worry the queen or the prince or princess any more.

"At night, when the queen and the prince and the princess were all safely sleeping in their cosy beds in their castle, a wise wizard appeared in a dream to each one of them. And this is what he said: 'You know the word *troll* is made up of a T an R an O and an L and another L and when you ever hear the word troll again you will know that the T stands for Together, the R for Remember, and the O for Our and the two LLs for Learning to Listen and this means that you now know the real meaning of the word *troll*: "Together we remember our learning to listen" to each other and for each other makes us feel safe inside and outside our castle. And the wise wizard said that the queen, the prince and the princess could feel safe and sense his presence and hear his wise words in times to come in their own special way, for he would always be there to guide them as they had learned that a troll just gets drunk and makes a lot of noise when you quickly find out that he cannot hurt you or bother you any more."

The counsellor extended this metaphor and spent four more counselling sessions combining play therapy with making castles and playing with puppets to enact the story of the metaphor of the dopey troll, the queen, the prince and the princess. During this time together they also experimented with inventing different endings to the stories and play. Many of these involved the troll being vanquished or banished from the queen's kingdom and the prince and princess inheriting the castle of their dreams. As a result, Jenny, Kenny and Davina became less bothered by the memories of 'their husband and father' and felt safe and more confident in their own house. Interestingly Kenny, who had started to wet the bed, stopped and began to introduce stories and drawings of castles, trolls and queens into his art lessons at school. Davina appeared less anxious in the presence of men and Jenny said what a stupid, pathetic and pitiful man her ex-husband had become. She had also started to venture out of the house more often with her children than she had in the months prior to coming for counselling.

Usefulness: the Test of Therapeutic Metaphors

●

We can now understand how to design and create therapeutic metaphors that can be useful to clients in counselling. At best we believe that metaphors are therapeutic in NLP counselling when the counsellor has an explicit strategy that can be used to design metaphors to suit the client and their situation. A therapeutic metaphor can have all of the elements of the seven-point strategy, but it need not have every one of them to have a therapeutic effect with clients. However, in our experience, the more elements of the seven-point strategy that are used to build the metaphor, the more likely the metaphor in use will turn out to be a therapeutic one. In general, therefore, a therapeutic metaphor in NLP counselling is judged in terms of its usefulness to the client.

Chapter 8

NLP COUNSELLING AND NLP TECHNOLOGY

The Gift of NLP Technology

●

Using NLP technology within counselling offers counsellors and clients a great gift. Neurolinguistic programming provides us with a set of useful models of human technology based on an infinite range of interpersonal and intrapersonal techniques. These NLP techniques can be adapted to each person according to their sensory representational systems in use and the linguistic, behavioural and thinking models of reality they have in operation at any one time.

In counselling NLP technology provides clients with more flexibility and choices in the way they live their lives and the outcomes they wish to experience in different situations. The use of NLP technologies by counsellors therefore provides us with a gift which we offer the clients we collaborate with in a working alliance within which counselling can take place. Here I would like to make clear my own preferred position as regards using NLP technology when counselling clients.

First, I use NLP technology as a way of creating and assisting the counselling processes involved in client change. Second, I prefer blending NLP techniques within the course of counselling sessions so that the whole may appear as a 'seamless robe' rather than items being added on like decorations on a birthday cake or afterthoughts like the balconies on some Byzantine buildings. Third, I am responsible for the direction of the counselling process and the NLP methods used with clients. As counselling progresses I encourage my clients to become innovative and experimental, developing self-management and personal change and control techniques of their own. Many of these are based on the NLP techniques they have learned in their counselling sessions with me.

I like using NLP technology in counselling and I find this works best when NLP methods or procedures can be skilfully blended with the orientation of the client and their current map of reality. In conducting NLP counselling, using NLP technology is rather like making a cake. For each client we need to be able to weigh up what their present state is, what they want and how they have been trying to get what they want. We need to know the sensory systems in use and not used by clients and the language patterns pursued in their interactions with the world they live in and the internal dialogues which prevent or help them to achieve personal outcomes to satisfy their personal maps of reality. We also need to find out if they are anchored to set patterns and stuck in the way they regard the meaning of events in their lives. Not least, NLP counsellors are curious about the degree of personal flexibility and the tasks clients engage in and the kinds of consequences these have for them in counselling and how they experience their world.

These are the essential ingredients that the NLP counsellor utilizes in each counselling session to empower clients to make the changes they wish to experience in their lives. The master baker has a clear outcome in mind: a well-blended, beautiful cake. The master NLP counsellor is also clear about his desired outcome — client change. The main gift of NLP technology in the hands of the counsellor is to increase the probability of creating the conditions where client change can take place. The rest is up to the client. As the great counsellor and psychotherapist Milton Erickson observed, "I don't think the therapist does anything except to say think about your problem in a favourable climate." A simple but very profound statement and one which we can now learn from in practical terms. For Erickson has encapsulated the essence of counselling with NLP. How do we create a favourable climate within which clients can think about their problems? Below we consider some criteria for using NLP technology in counselling to create the conditions for change. I have found they help to foster a favourable therapeutic climate with clients.

Rapport First, Last and Always
●

Earlier we saw how rapport involves reaching out to each and every client who comes for counselling. In NLP counselling, rapport can be conceived of as those specific states that increase the clients' responsiveness and participation in their environment. I am using the term 'environment' here intentionally in a broad way to encompass the counsellor, the counselling clinic, the buildings and the different associations clients may have at any point in the counselling process. I do not see it as useful or even desirable to abandon the term 'rapport' in favour of 'transference', since the observed dynamics of counsellor–client interactions suggest that rapport is present regardless of whether transference is positive or negative. Rapport may thus be considered a more comprehensive construct. In NLP counselling, therefore, we should think of transference as being included within the realm of rapport and in some instances being considered simply as an extension of rapport.

Regarding the creation of rapport, some clients seem to make it easy for the NLP counsellor. Others appear to make it difficult. At least that is something many counsellors would have us believe. I used to believe it myself — until I found that nothing is wasted in counselling. Milton Erickson is reported as saying that all he ever did was to point the client in the right direction and head for home. There is a story that illustrates this very well. One day, when Erickson was a young man, a farmer had a horse that bolted and ran miles away from the farm. Efforts to force the horse back failed. Erickson is said to have simply got on the horse's back and pointed him in the right direction and let the horse do the rest — and it found its own way back. Similarly rapport is not a forcing of effort by the NLP counsellor to go in a particular direction; it is merely joining the client in such a way that you can go in the same direction. When you can do this the client has started pacing her 'journey home'.

Another way of understanding rapport is found in the Taoist proverb cited earlier: the longest journey begins with the first step. The first step is made by the client when she decides to come for counselling. When she arrives at the counselling clinic she may be subject to one or a mixture of any number of emotional, mental or physical conditions. She may behave agreeably and be compliant. She may be relieved to see a counsellor. She may blame you or hate you. She may be unsure what to expect from counselling. You may be her first chance of help. She may see you as her last hope. Sometimes it seems as if rapport can never be built, for a variety of curious reasons: the client is resistant. The client is too aggressive. The client is unable to communicate. The counsellor and client are locked in so-called 'transference and counter-transference problems'. The possibilities are endless, but the principle is the same. The counsellor claims that the client cannot build rapport or that she is presenting herself in counselling in such a way that it is impossible to create rapport.

Counselling with NLP helps to overcome these apparent difficulties in building rapport with clients. Providing the counsellor is flexible enough, rapport can be achieved with most clients. Creating rapport has nothing to do with liking clients in counselling. It involves our being flexible enough to adapt to them sufficiently well for counselling to take place.

Counsellor and Client Orientation

In my experience as an NLP counsellor, one of the first things clients do with me and I do with them is to engage in orienting towards each other. Interestingly, the *Concise Oxford Dictionary* defines orientation as 'Orienting (oneself) or being oriented; relative position; faculty by which birds etc find their way home from a distance.' It is essential that the client and counsellor orient towards each other within the first counselling session and thereafter in each subsequent counselling session. Like birds in flight they need to be with each other on the same flight path so they can navigate their way through the counselling process and find their way 'home'. Sometimes the orientation stage of counselling with NLP will be straightforward: we match what the client says; we use similar language and reflect back to the client how we experience her feelings, thoughts and actions; we breathe in a similar way so as to create rapport and an accurate reflection of empathy; we use a tonality which helps us to tune into the voice and interests of our clients; and we can use the kinds of emphasis and themes of conversation which cement the counselling relationship. All of these NLP techniques increase the probability that we will develop powerful rapport and create a shared orientation to the work we do with clients. The NLP counsellor has the responsibility of aligning himself with his clients and facilitating mutual orientation.

In many cases clients and counsellors are quickly attuned. But what about those clients who are not readily agreeable to working on their personal difficulties with their counsellors? I have found that this is where NLP technology can be particularly useful. Even when the counsellor has a difficult or resistant client, a satisfactory mutual orientation can be achieved and counselling can proceed.

Consider some of the following instances of the counsellor–client orientation. Which clients were accommodating and compliant, ready to orient themselves with the counsellor? Which ones were not? How did the counsellor use his NLP skills to achieve a satisfactory orientation with the client?

Case Example One: Maria

COUNSELLOR: Please come in, Maria. Sit anywhere you like. Now tell me what brings you here today.

MARIA: Thanks ... well, it all started three years ago. I met this married man ... and ever since ...

Case Example Two: Stephen

COUNSELLOR: Thank you for coming, Stephen [*gestures to Stephen to sit down*].

STEPHEN: I never wanted to come here. I was forced by my brother. I don't want to be here.

COUNSELLOR: That's right, Stephen, you want to be somewhere else.

STEPHEN: Yes, I do ... away from here ...

COUNSELLOR: Somewhere, where you can ...

STEPHEN: Be on my own ... and think things out.

COUNSELLOR: About ..?

STEPHEN: My illness ... it's getting me down. I mean my fear of ...

COUNSELLOR: You know I am here and you can be safe and still work things out on your own.

STEPHEN: It ... is ... so ... hard ... for me ... [breathes a big sigh].

COUNSELLOR: It must be difficult to soften how you think about your fear right now.

STEPHEN: [starts to cry, sighs and pauses and then is silent for some time with his head inclined downwards]: I don't know why I am crying like a baby ... I should not, but ...

COUNSELLOR: But ...

STEPHEN: I feel a little bit better ... [carries on crying].

COUNSELLOR: Mmm ... mmm ... mmm [makes comforting noises].

STEPHEN: I will go now, but I would like to come back ...

Case Example Three: Lorraine

COUNSELLOR: Hello again, Lorraine.

LORRAINE: Hi [stares angrily at counsellor].

COUNSELLOR: Last time we worked together you said you wanted to lighten up, and be more relaxed and chill out with your son — is that right?

LORRAINE: Yes and no [looks at the counsellor and bares her teeth, rolls her upper lip over her teeth and growls at the counsellor].

COUNSELLOR: I wonder if the 'yes' part of you is the angry part, or is it the 'no' part? Or maybe your 'yes' and 'no' parts are both angry?

LORRAINE: [Pauses for a few moments; anger fades from her face and tone]: I feel different, but I don't know why.

COUNSELLOR: Lorraine, you know it is OK not to know and you can still feel different ... You and I do not have answers to everything we face together ...

LORRAINE: No one ever said that to me before. I would have to think about it ...

COUNSELLOR: OK, think about it ...

LORRAINE: Mmm, I'm thinking [Her eyes go up left, then right, then down to the right].

LORRAINE: Mmm ... you are [emphasizes both words 'you' and 'are' with an increased pitch at the end of each word] ... And as you are thinking, what ...?

LORRAINE: Lots of pictures. And feelings ... and pictures and back to feelings. It's weird ... It is ... like these are racing back and forwards to me, coming up to my face and then vanishing ...

COUNSELLOR: Still pictures, moving pictures, coloured pictures — what kind?

LORRAINE: Coloured and moving [*her breathing is fast*].

COUNSELLOR: That's good, Lorraine. So what happens when you bring the pictures close to you?

LORRAINE: Yes ... I get mad and angry. I want to hurt him. Joe ... my son ... [*her face flushes*].

COUNSELLOR: Now go back to your 'yes' and 'no'. What do they tell you now?

LORRAINE: Ah ... Yes, I am angry with Joe. He is so aggressive to me and the 'no' makes me aggressive as well. Because I don't think I should put up with his attitude any more.

COUNSELLOR: OK. Now, when you take the pictures and put them farther away from you, what happens? Do that now?

LORRAINE: Er .. well, less annoyed ... I'm still not happy with him.

COUNSELLOR: Can you dim the colours down or make them black and white? Can you do that?

LORRAINE: Yes ... mmm ... black and white.

COUNSELLOR: What are you getting?

LORRAINE: The feeling, it's sort of neutral, just neutral ... kind of calmer.

COUNSELLOR: Lorraine, now put 'yes' in there. How is that?

LORRAINE: Yes, still calm.

COUNSELLOR: That's good. Do that ten or more times. Just keep running it through like that.

LORRAINE: Mmm. Yes [*her face colour is natural, her breathing relaxed*].

COUNSELLOR: [*now breathing in rhythm with Lorraine*]: Do the same for 'no'. How is that ... when you do it?

LORRAINE: The strong feelings again, the pictures closer, in colour and sharper, brighter.

COUNSELLOR: OK. So just go back to 'yes' and 'no', will you? And now run them through and see what goes on ...

LORRAINE: Oh ... It's clearer now. Yes, clearer.

COUNSELLOR: What do you see?

LORRAINE: I see I do love Joe strongly, but I am not going to go on accepting *his* problems and making them mine any more.

COUNSELLOR: You can see it is clear now ... One more thing, Lorraine. Think about your son and bare your teeth. Put your lip like this [*he demonstrates*].

LORRAINE: I can't do that. I don't feel the same any more.

COUNSELLOR: Good, Lorraine. You have done a lot of good work today.

LORRAINE: Yes ...

COUNSELLOR: Maybe ... you can be interested in how you can do something important for yourself outside this room ...?

LORRAINE: I think I can ...

The Shared Orientation

When we share the orientation of the client in counselling we are working with the client's map of reality. We use the sensory representational language of the client and their eye movements, body language and tonality to create the conditions whereby we achieve mutual orientation.

As can be seen from the case examples, each client can be slightly different from any other. NLP counsellors need to be flexible enough to adapt to the demands made on them to become attuned to their clients. A successful orientation increases rapport. Successful rapport increases the opportunities for shared orientation towards the counselling process. Without it client change is unlikely to take place. Fortunately the sensory, linguistic and behavioural feedback provided to the counsellor by the client gives him the 'raw data' — the information to which a shared orientation can be facilitated and blended into the counselling process by the NLP counsellor.

Even the most difficult and uncompliant clients can be brought into a shared orientation towards counselling by the counsellor. Milton Erickson showed how this could be done with a restless, unco-operative client who came to his clinic. The client insisted that Erickson could not help him, that no one could, and he rapidly paced back and forth between two chairs in Erickson's office. Erickson simply asked if the man would mind if he spoke to him as he paced back and forth in the room. What Erickson did next was the mark of a genius. He spoke in time with the rate at which the client paced up and down the room. And he also described what the client was doing. So, for instance, when the client was near one chair Erickson would say, "Now you are near the chair and when you get there you can turn around and walk to the other chair. Now turn back and walk back again." Eventually Erickson slowed down his rate of speaking. In line with this, the client slowed down his walking until he was next to one chair and sat in it. There are many different aspects to this story, but for the NLP counsellor it nicely illustrates how even with extremely 'resistant' or 'difficult' clients, it is possible to obtain a mutual orientation and rapport.

The Counsellor-Client Fit

●

In my view it is imperative that the counsellor and client obtain a satisfactory 'fit' in their *working relationship* together. The better the fit in counselling, the more likely unshakeable rapport can be achieved and sustained. The poorer the fit between them, the shallower and more fragile the rapport. In the latter case the processes and products of counselling tend to culminate in undesirable results for both counsellor and client. In NLP counselling a good fit results in rapport and retrieval of useful information, informed choices and change. A bad fit prevents or breaks an accepted working relationship between clients and their counsellors.

NLP counsellors consciously pursue the formation of a good fit between themselves and their clients. Sometimes they may wish to adjust the counsellor–client fit to increase or decrease the tension in the relationship between counsellor and client. At other times they may wish to strengthen it, or facilitate new choices with the client, or to end the counselling session. When they wish to increase the soundness of the counsellor–client fit to realize a particular outcome they can encourage the use of specific NLP techniques such as rapport building and matching and mirroring.

NLP counselling provides the counsellor with many ways of creating the conditions for client change, based on what Carl Rogers has described as the working relationship between the counsellor and client. This is what productive NLP counselling is about. It is based upon a shared experience of *working,* whereby the counsellor and client establish implicitly or explicitly the work to be done during and between sessions and after their time set aside for counselling activity. The process and product of this working time are heavily dependent on the quality of the counsellor–client relationship.

Personal Information

As we have seen, within the client–counsellor relationship there is an exchange of information — personal information: information that is personal to the client and is shared with the counsellor. The counsellor also shares personal information about himself. For the counsellor–client relationship to work there has to be an ebbing and flowing, a sharing and caring, a mutual agreement to share personal information. The main focus of attention is on information about the client. It is upon the personal information of the client that NLP counselling acts and changes. Where the client is flexible, willing and in rapport with the counsellor, she is usually prepared to risk sharing herself with the counsellor and the counsellor shares himself with her. Now the pertinent issue for NLP counselling rests on the kind of information that is shared between counsellor and client within the counselling relationship. We have considered above how sometimes clients have too much information that they are trying to retrieve to solve their problems. At other times they have too little. On other occasions again they need to sift, sort and reorder their personal information in such a way that they can experience more satisfying outcomes in their lives.

Practical Counselling Skills (Bailey, 1993) described the way clients in counselling try to organize and make sense of their personal information in their attempts to help themselves:

A bit like an amateur juggler, they have all the balls they need to perform an impressive juggling act. However, they do not know how to keep all the balls in the air. They somehow can't quite discover the secret of how to co-ordinate the throwing of the balls, the movement of the hands, the balance of the body with the concentration on keeping the sequence of movements going so the balls do not collide or just simply fall down. One of the fascinating things about jugglers is that they start with the most that they can handle with ease, and add to it, gradually and progressively building up so that they juggle more and more balls and still make it look easy. I find that clients who have too much information, and are troubled in some way special to them, often have something in common. They are trying to juggle too many balls at once."

(Bailey, 1993)

Counselling and NLP Information Retrieval Skills

Counselling with NLP allows us to gain access to the personal information of the client. Information retrieval skills consist of questioning and calibrating the present state of clients, and formulating the way in which clients are using information internally and externally in the patterns of their behaviour.

As well as gaining access to the 'hot' or 'cold' information clients may be using to map out their sensory experiences and the way they represent them in the different forms of language they use, NLP technology helps us to work with the size and structure of the client's personal information. We find out from the client if she constructs her experience in small bits or big chunks of personal information.

Chunking Up and Chunking Down with Personal Information

In NLP counselling we refer to this use of personal information as 'chunking up' and 'chunking down'. Why should this be important for counsellors and clients in counselling? First of all, we can use it to understand how rapport can be built and strengthened with clients. Second, we can plot the structure of the kinds of personal information clients bring to counselling. Third, we can discover the limitations clients put on their choices and current experiences and the way they wish to experience the future outcomes they want in their lives. From this we can begin to utilize the personal information of clients to expand their cognitive maps of reality and enrich their range of choices. The sensitive use of chunking up or chunking down the personal information of clients thus plays a central part in NLP counselling. It helps to change the reality of the client.

Logical Levels and Chunking

Chunking is based on Bertrand Russell's theory of logical types, brilliantly extended in 1964 by Gregory Bateson in his paper, 'The Logical Categories of Learning and Communication'. Essentially Bateson expounded the thesis that the way people learn takes place on many different *logical levels*. As Charlotte Bretto, the distinguished communicator on the use of NLP, describes it:

> On one level, I learn how to do all the kinds of procedures included in addition, multiplication and subtraction, without understanding how they work. On the next level, I learn how these calculations work, in a way that allows me to proceed on my own to learn how, for example, to do division. Learning on the next level would, then, allow me to understand how I learned to do these calculations. This is derived from Russell's theory that 'a class of classes cannot be one of the classes which are its members: that a name is not the thing named'.
>
> (Bretto, 1988)

In NLP counselling, the more clients can move from one logical level to the next, and the next, the more variety and flexibility they will have available to them in different life contexts. By doing this, clients can extend their repertoire of coping abilities and increase their range of personal learning and survival strategies. Chunking allows counsellors to open up and move through many levels of learning with their clients. This is one reason why those counsellors using NLP in their work often encourage their clients to realize they are 'learning on many levels'. Clients can engage in chunking up or chunking down. The more logical levels they can move through, the more choices that are potentially accessible to them to change their reality and the way they experience it.

Chunking Up

Chunking is thus a central part of counselling with NLP. When clients or counsellors are chunking up information they are moving towards speaking in more general terms, and towards more inclusive classes of things, objects, people and situations, and any thoughts, feelings or behaviours they believe go along with the representations they make about reality through their senses. Chunking up is often associated with what has become known as the Meta model of communication (named after Milton Erickson). This is where larger and larger pieces of information are provided by clients. Clearly chunking up serves many purposes in NLP counselling. It is often useful in helping the counsellor to discover the belief systems currently used by clients and the personal meanings and lexical referencing attached to their personal information.

Case Example Four: Chunking Up

CLIENT: Each time he nods his head like that it annoys me intensely.

COUNSELLOR: What is his head nodding like that an example of?

CLIENT: It is as clear as day to me — he hates me ... because ... of his personality.

COUNSELLOR: So nodding his head like this [he demonstrates] is a sign of hate?

CLIENT: Yes, the way you did it right then — that is it. He hates me when he does that.

COUNSELLOR: OK. I can see that now. And if I nod my head, what then?

CLIENT: Well, maybe you don't hate me, maybe you just ...

COUNSELLOR: I just ...

CLIENT: You disapprove ...

COUNSELLOR: I see ... it is to you my way of showing I disapprove of you ... Is that right?

CLIENT: Yes ... that is true ...

COUNSELLOR: Mmm ... mmm ...

Chunking Down

In chunking down, clients or counsellors are engaging in working with smaller and smaller classes of items, things or objects. The NLP counsellor chunks down when specificity is required to clarify or shift the emphasis in the personal information being retrieved by clients during counselling sessions. Usually referred to as challenging the meta-model, this is where the NLP counsellor skilfully questions clients with the intention of moving from general to more specific chunks of personal information located at the sensory level of representation. Meta-model challenging by the NLP counsellor therefore involves him in empowering the client to retrieve specific aspects of her personal map of reality.

Case Example Five: Chunking Down

CLIENT: I know I just have to improve my relationship with Bernie.

COUNSELLOR: What stops you from improving it?

CLIENT: He is so aggressive it makes me frightened ...

COUNSELLOR: Of what?

CLIENT: Oh, everything!

COUNSELLOR: Everything? [*He re-emphasizes what the client has said in a questioning tone*]

CLIENT: Well, nearly everything ...

COUNSELLOR: I mean, are you feeling frightened right now?

CLIENT: No ... not at this precise moment.

COUNSELLOR: How do you feel at this moment?

CLIENT: Er ... I would have to think about it ...

COUNSELLOR: That is OK. You can think about it ...

CLIENT: Mmm ... at this moment I am in control —— no real feelings of fear [*her eyes look up to left and then down right*].

COUNSELLOR: That is really interesting. So what have you got instead?

CLIENT: I am kind of comfortable [*her eyes look down right and then stare unfocused straight ahead*].

COUNSELLOR: So you feel in control and sort of comfortable right now — is that right?

CLIENT: Yes, that's right. Yes, right. That is how I feel just now.

COUNSELLOR: So there are situations when you don't feel frightened?

CLIENT: I agree. That is true. I just forgot and now I remember.

COUNSELLOR: That's good. Now, as you sit there and remember, what other specific situations come to mind where you feel comfortable and relaxed?

CLIENT: Quite a few. I can see them as I am talking to you.

COUNSELLOR: Which specific one or particular theme comes out from those scenes flashing past in your mind?

CLIENT: There is a special one. It is where I stood my ground and people listened to me.

COUNSELLOR: That is great ... so stick with that for a moment ... and study it closely now and notice ... what it is you are saying, how you are saying it ... what is your body doing and how do you succeed in doing all of that?

CLIENT: Mmm ... Yes ... I can see it all again. I get this secure feeling this feeling I can do it ... anyway ... so why be frightened? The fear is smaller than it was ...

COUNSELLOR: Wonderful! You can do it. Just allow that secure feeling to grow as the fear gets smaller and smaller [*he pauses*]. What are the words you are using? Notice how they are sounding as they come out of your mouth and notice how you have changed ... and you are doing that in every detail ... That's right — in every detail ... You can take your time or speed it up as you remember how relaxed and comfortable you feel ...

Nominalizations and Specifications

●

Nominalizations

Nominalizations and specifications are used a great deal in counselling with NLP.

Nominalizations are those general linguistic exchanges between counsellors and clients which are very general in nature. Words such as defensive, bewildered, confused, beneficial, enjoyment, annoyed, unbearable, attractive, depressed, anxious, relieved, terrified and confident are all nominalizations.

A nominalization is created when we communicate by transforming a verb into an abstract noun and express it 'as if' it were a noun and referred to a concrete entity. Thus a client may describe themselves as 'stressed and depressed'. There is a saying in NLP counselling that nicely encapsulates the use of nominalizations: linguistically, 'if you can't put it in a bucket' it is a nominalization. Nominalizations are usually present when chunking up is occurring in counselling. If you quickly scan the case example of chunking up, you should be able to detect at least five nominalizations used by the client.

Specifications

Specification in NLP is the converse of nominalization. Here the counsellor is progressively refining personal information clients bring to counselling sessions into smaller and more precise pieces. Rudyard Kipling captured the essence of chunking down:

> I have six honest serving men
> (They taught me all I knew)
> Their names are What and Why and When
> And How and Where and Who.

The chunking down case example shows some of the many ways that counsellors use NLP chunking skills with clients. We need to know where problems are experienced. We need to know what happens and what does not happen. We need to know when it does and when it does not happen, with whom, where and how it takes place. Some counsellors also work with their clients towards an understanding of why their difficulties have happened. Some do not. In NLP counselling, when the 'why' question raises itself, my personal preference is to work mostly in the present tense: why a person believes something is happening now and how this can be changed. In NLP counselling, chunking down sometimes leads to the 'why' question. Curiously, understanding why something happens or does not happen, when pursued with appropriate questioning, can often help to elicit the core beliefs of clients.

These core beliefs flip us back to chunking up. For instance, when a client is asked why they continue to live in the same house as their partner who regularly and frequently beats them, they may say "Because I am a bad person" or "I suppose I deserve it." The point I wish to make here is that, when we are using NLP technology, chunking up and chunking down both serve a particular purpose at different points in the counselling process. They are not fixed points or antagonistic to one another, but should be appreciated as being complementary, alternating, ebbing and flowing and intertwining during the counselling that takes place between counsellors and clients.

Conclusion
●

The usefulness of NLP technology in counselling is almost limitless. Where the limits lie depends largely on the ingenuity, innovativeness and flexibility of each counsellor. Every individual client, couple or family in counselling is unique. The personal maps each has will vary from person to person and family to family. NLP technology does not bind us to a slavish following of one particular theory: we can use NLP technology with many theories of counselling. Knowing this offers us the opportunity to mould our counselling practice alongside the utilization of NLP skills with and for each client. Adopting NLP technology in counselling empowers us in the pursuit of understanding the individuality of clients. It allows us a greater freedom and potential flexibility when we engage in the enterprise of helping. For the client it promises one other means by which new choices can be made in the way they live and experience their personal reality.

Chapter 9

CHOOSING AND CHOICES

Tasks

●

Tasks are an essential part of counselling with NLP. A great deal of the time the counsellor is engaged on tasks, and so is the client. Some of these tasks are explicit and are the responsibility of both counsellor and client. Building rapport, creating and maintaining confidentiality, calibrating client states and identifying the sensory representational systems in use by clients and the kinds of language predicates and experiences they bring about are all part of the tasks engaged in during the counselling process.

A fundamental task of the NLP counsellor is to identify client tasks, obtain client commitment to tasks and to monitor them throughout the counselling contact with the client. The client also has the task of choosing whether or not to become involved in the counselling she is being offered and how far she will take charge of the choices and changes she may wish to make and experience in her life.

Tasks form the backbone of NLP counselling. They support everything the client and counsellor do in counselling, from beginning to ending their mutual involvement in the counselling process. Without tasks we struggle to make progress. With them, we may still struggle, but at least we struggle with the client to find the strength to make changes, or at least to begin to move towards having different experiences from the problems they bring to counselling. Clearly, then, there are tasks for the client and for the counsellor.

Part of the difficulty for the counsellor in NLP counselling, as in other forms of counselling, is deciding what tasks need to be pursued and knowing when they have been completed with and by the client (see Table 10).

Table 10: Guidelines for tasks in NLP counselling	
Counsellor	**Client**
Establishing credentials/confidentiality	Being satisfied with credentials/confidentiality
Calibrating client states.	Past/present/future states
Matching and mirroring to build trust/rapport	Reciprocating trust/rapport
Identifying eye accessing movements	Engaging in eye accessing
Noticing the use of specific sensory/representational systems	Utilizing specific sensory representational systems
Assessing client use of linguistic predicates	Expressing linguistic predicates
Retrieving personal information	Searching for information
Challenging the use of generalization/deletion/distortion	Challenging own use of generalization/deletion/distortion
Establishing anchoring and re-anchoring	Anchoring and re-anchoring
Framing and reframing client experiences	Experiencing within a frame of reference
Setting and pursuing personal outcomes	Selecting personal outcomes
Working with well-formed outcomes	Choosing well-formed outcomes. Rehearsing personal outcomes.
Utilizing client resources	Releasing personal resources
Maintaining/reviewing/changing client patterns and strategy	Maintaining/reviewing/changing personal patterns and strategy

Calibration and Clients

Calibration has a special place in the practice of counselling using NLP techniques. It involves measuring and, at best, is the accurate recognition of the state of another person at any particular time. It involves the counsellor in identifying the verbal and non-verbal state of the client. Also the counsellor assesses the tonality of his client's voice and the kinds of words and meanings attached to the concerns of the client. The way the client sits, the emphasis on specific words and phrases, the repetition of themes and the kinds of deletions, distortions and generalizations used by clients are all presented to the counsellor during counselling and all contribute to the calibration of the client.

When they first talk on the phone, when they first meet, and afterwards at all subsequent counselling sessions, the counsellor has the opportunity and indeed the responsibility of calibrating the different states of his client at different points in the counselling process. The counsellor using NLP techniques has the specific task of calibrating ('reading') their client.

When we are calibrating the various states of our clients well, we can, so to speak, read them like a book. Over time we can get to know them very well. Sometimes it takes only a session or two to read our clients and their inner states. On other occasions, or with a different client, we can take longer to learn to read them well. With some clients we can tell right away and get an accurate gauge of how they feel and the kinds of thinking and language patterns they use and bring to counselling. The counsellor can calibrate the words that are associated with particular states such as feeling good, bad, anxious, angry and depressed, or those which open up or close down the progress of rapport and fresh choices to better manage or overcome their personal problems. Some clients change their state many times in counselling sessions. Others seem immobilized into one specific state, and this can be one of the reasons they have come to counselling.

Table 11 lists some ways to cue yourself in to calibrating clients and the states they are experiencing.

Table 11: Calibrating client states	
1	Notice clients' faces and how their skin colour changes at different points in the counselling session.
2	Observe the eye movements of your clients.
3	Pay attention to the speed of eye movement: when it increases and decreases as clients are talking to you.
4	Identify other movements such as those of the head, hands and fingers and what they are doing when particular topics are raised during counselling.
5	Be aware of larger movements such as those of the legs and arms, and swaying, bobbing or turning that clients engage in when talking about their 'problems'.
6	Listen for the kinds of words, phrases and emphases used by clients.
7	Register the preferred sensory representational systems of clients and the types of metaphor they express through their language when talking to you.
8	Focus on the changes of state in clients when 'hot spots' and 'cool spots' are faced together in counselling: the concerns which produce the raw heat of emotion and those which leave the client unmoved and composed, calm and confident.
9	Check what 'time' mode clients are engaging in through the tenses they use in counselling. Be alert and notice if they are talking in the present, past or future tense about their personal difficulties.
10	Decide when clients are associating with their problems and when they are dissociating themselves from them in their own particular way. Another way of understanding this kind of calibration is to be vigilant for those times when clients are 'in' their problems and emotionally re-experiencing them, and those times when they 'stand back' from their problems and talk about them from a distance.

The Importance of Calibration

There are some similarities between other forms of counselling and the NLP counselling techniques of calibrating the different states of clients. The person-centred counsellor is sensitive to clients and their present reality. He emphasizes the 'now' of the client. The reality therapist addresses and works with the needs of the client. The Gestalt counsellor resonates with the immediate gestalt of clients and the transactional analysis counsellor assesses the current and changing ego states of clients in their journey through counselling.

NLP counselling is complementary to these schools of counselling. However, at the same time, NLP counselling is very different. The difference is that the NLP counsellor intentionally sets out to discover the current state of clients when they first come to counselling and at different points during the counselling process. This is done through calibrating the way clients use their sensory representational systems to create their reality and report on it through their spoken language and non-language behaviours. In this way rapport can be accomplished.

Calibration and Rapport

One of the essential outcomes for an NLP counsellor in counselling is to create the conditions where clients can entertain the kinds of changes they may want to make in their lives. A more subtle point is that, by accurately calibrating the differing states of clients, the NLP counsellor is in a better position to make informed decisions about the most *appropriate way* to create rapport. He can then utilize the rapport as a base on which to obtain information about the client's habits and what limits her or prevents her from making new choices and resolving her problems. Carefully calibrating client states therefore plays a large part in forming the foundations for therapeutic change.

We engage in careful calibration of clients' habits, feelings and thoughts. We pay attention. We take an interest, and notice, gauge and monitor client behaviours, because this provides the psychological information which enables us to help clients change their habits and consider new choices.

Harnessed by Habits

●

In many ways we are creatures of habit. Most of our habits we have chosen at some stage in our lives. We walk and talk in a certain way. We talk, move our lips and head, and develop other habitual mannerisms such as shaking the hands of clients on greeting or on parting.

These typical examples are usually satisfactory and they work for us. We keep using them and they become habitual. However sometimes they become so habitual that we no longer notice what we are doing, saying or feeling or what triggers our behaviours, thoughts and feelings, that can result in painful, unwanted and undesirable experiences. When this is the case, we are prisoners of our own habits. Many of the clients we see in our clinics are prisoners of their habits. They do things, feel things, think things; and so do what they do not want to do. Counsellors from many different schools must see clients like these in their clinics all the time.

Anchoring and Habits

●

In NLP terms these clients are anchored to their problems. An anchor is heavy. It holds you in one place. It takes quite an effort to lift it — unless you have some powerful lifting gear. An anchor may be new, bright and shiny or it may be old and rusty.

These and many other aspects of the anchor metaphor apply to the way clients are anchored to their experiences: their reactions; their sensory representations; the language they use; the way they think, feel and behave.

Moreover, it is not just the experience that can be anchored to specific situations; or situations with particular themes in them. Clients can also be anchored to the way they habitually *use* a specific sensory representational system and this can create wanted or unwanted experiences for them. Clients are also often anchored to particular strategies of feeling, thinking and behaving in different situations and with particular individuals. One of the tasks for the NLP counsellor is to discover which anchors the clients is bonded to and those to which they wish to remain bonded.

The counsellor has another task: to *re-anchor* clients in different ways so they can experience the sensory representations, thoughts, feelings and behaviour they want in their lives. In short, the NLP counsellor's task here is to enable clients to change old habits for new.

Case Example One: Anchored to Mixed Feelings

In this case Janet is unclear about her mixed feelings for Philip and has some reservations about whether or not she wants to live with him any more. They have been together two years, but in the past six months Janet has felt 'up and down' with her partner and she cannot quite see how this is affecting her so much.

COUNSELLOR: So, if I have understood you, Janet, you are unsure of your feelings for Philip and whether you want to stay with him any more.

JANET: Yes, I feel so angry and confused about my situation and even the sound of his name makes me cringe [*she shakes her shoulders and turns down her mouth and shakes her head from side to side*].

COUNSELLOR: If I have heard you right, Janet ... I mean, if I pull back just for a second and tune-in my mind ... that is how you feel right now ... Can you recall when you first met Philip?

JANET: Yes, I can very clearly ... mmm I can [*her face changes colour, the muscle tone softens and her voice lightens*].

COUNSELLOR: Janet, when you focus on that image of Philip, just notice what immediately springs to mind.

JANET: I feel different ... It was 1994 and we met on a package holiday ... in Spain. Phil's sister Lorraine was there ... she arranged a date for us .... He was ... different then ... more carefree ...

COUNSELLOR: Carefree ... if I had a video of Phil being carefree, what would he look like?

JANET: Well, he had this great big smile — it stretched right across his face ... [*As Janet describes this her face breaks into a big grin*].

COUNSELLOR: That's good Janet ... Now really take a good look at that smile ... the shape of his mouth, the colour of his skin ... the shape of his face, his eyes ... the curve of his mouth ...

JANET: Yes, I really miss that smile ... it gives me a good feeling ... it felt safe being with Phil.

COUNSELLOR: You can hold that smile and put it in the corner over there [points to the back of Janet's head] so you can get it back again any time you want to. Can you do that?

JANET: That's fine by me. I can do that.

COUNSELLOR: Janet, I wonder if you would like to do something else right now ... Get a picture of Philip's face now and what do you get?

JANET: Ugh ... I don't like what I see ... ugh ...

COUNSELLOR: You don't like that ... what are you getting now?

JANET: He is sneering at me .... You know, his mouth is like he wants to spit something out ... and his eyes and nose are screwed up ... when he looks at me ... A kind of look you get when you smell something that is rotting and horrible ... Maybe it's disgust ... But that is what I see ... now.

COUNSELLOR: So let's see if I have got this right, Janet ... You have good feelings when you focus on Phil's smile and you get unpleasant and unwanted feelings when Philip looks at you now ...

JANET: That is true ... You know, before today I never gave a second thought about how much the expression on his face could affect me.

Analysis

What were the anchors in this case? How did these change? What were the feelings they produced for Janet? What specific sensory representational systems was she using? Did you notice the predicates she used that matched her experiences? What did the counsellor do? When was the counsellor pacing and leading? Let us consider these and other questions.

Janet was anchored to the expressions on Philip's face. She was also anchored to different feelings that went along with these expressions. It was also noticeable that when he wore a certain 'look' she regarded him as 'Philip' and she had a kinaesthetic reaction that gave her feelings she did not like: she cringed at the sound of his name. She 'heard' his voice in a variety of ways, depending on the expression he wore on his face, and this accounted for many of the different feelings she had about him. At the same time she used her visual representation to signal to her what kind of feelings were anchored to his frown or his smile. When he was smiling he was no longer 'Philip' but 'Phil' and Janet felt more relaxed and happier when he was carefree. On this point Janet showed to the counsellor that she could call up a representation of her partner that was anchored in the past to good feelings. This was the anchor for Phil. She also demonstrated that she frequently used an auditory–visual representation based on her more recent perceptions of her partner's facial expression. This gave her unwanted feelings. This was the anchor for Philip. She also used appropriate visual and auditory predicates during the counselling session and these were reciprocated by the NLP counsellor.

Case Example Two: Re-anchoring

Sometimes clients need to have different feelings about a situation they frequently have to face: it may be once a month, once a week or even each day. Counsellors can help clients to do this by using an NLP technique called 're-anchoring'.

Ben, a 32-year-old, had the habit of blushing every time he saw a woman and tried to ask her out for drinks or invite her to a party. He wanted to get rid of the habit as it was ruining his social life. His friends had also started to mock him in front of the opposite sex and call him 'Ben the beetroot boy'. At these times Ben would suddenly flush and everyone seemed to erupt in laughter.

BEN: It is just so bad ... at college ... I can't tell you how anxious and tongue-tied I get and all because my face goes as red as a traffic light when I see a woman I fancy ... It happens all the time ...

COUNSELLOR: You say there is a kind of sequence here, Ben. Is that right?

BEN: Yes ... I have had it for years ...

COUNSELLOR: So how does the sequence go again?

BEN: As I say, I see a woman, I say to myself I fancy her and then slam! I'm beetroot red ... It happens so quickly, like automatically ...

COUNSELLOR: That's good ...

BEN: Good? What do you mean?

COUNSELLOR: I mean knowing that you know how you do it ... Could you please do it for me now?

BEN: No way! I can't do it now ... I can't, even though I try.

COUNSELLOR: That's OK. Try harder. Really try. Notice what happens. Are you really trying to blush? Really try for me.

BEN: I'm trying the hardest I can, but I can't do it ...

COUNSELLOR: That is great, Ben. Now, what do you make of that?

BEN: I am surprised ... really surprised ... Funny — the harder I tried the less I could do it ... But with a woman I would still cringe and go red again ...

COUNSELLOR: Ben, you really surprised me. Well done ... Thank yourself, why don't you? You know, you did something special there. I wonder if you can imagine what it was ... and keep that to yourself ... it's your secret?

BEN: No, I would like to tell you.

COUNSELLOR: That's all right. Tell me then.

BEN: I must know ... er know ...

COUNSELLOR: You know ...?

BEN: That's it. I know how to blush ...

COUNSELLOR: And ...?

BEN: I must know how *not* to blush as well [*his face momentarily has a look of discovery and relief on it*].

COUNSELLOR: You're right. You do know how to blush and how not to. Would you like to allow yourself to not blush more often?

BEN: Definitely

COUNSELLOR: If you work with me on this ... that would be all right with you, would it, Ben?

BEN: I want to ... you know I want to ...

COUNSELLOR: OK, Ben. Here is what I would like you to do ... You know how not to blush and that is a very clever thing to know; and there are times for blushing and not blushing and you can save your blushing times for those other times when you need to blush. But right now you can allow yourself to do less blushing each time you ... think about it. Think about a time when you felt really good ... let me know when you have got that ...

BEN: I have got one ... it's summer ... a favourite place I go to when I want to feel good ... It's near a forest in ...

COUNSELLOR: You can tell me all the details or you can keep it to yourself ... Nobody needs to know ... It's OK ... Now you are in this forest ... I would like you to pay attention to anything that allows you to strengthen that good feeling ... It may be the colours of the forest, the trees, the special light, or you could just listen to the sounds of the birds and the kinds of comforting and confident thoughts you have. Just make sure you are getting what you want from this experience.

BEN: Mmm. I am getting colours, greens and browns, and the light is kind of pale and soothing and there are birds singing. It's like a kind of heaven ... Mmm ... I like being here ... The leaves are so beautiful. Mmm ...

COUNSELLOR: That's good, Ben. Really good ... You can make those experiences happen ... really ... Stay with them ... just ... let yourself intensify the light — not too much, but enough for you to discover what is happening to you — and breathe in the air and let yourself amplify the sounds and really study the way those leaves and their colours are brilliant in their own way. Each and every one is different and you can have the same good feelings every time you hear the birds or see them on the branches of the trees, bobbing up and down on the leaves and twigs ... Go with that. It's easy for you now ...

BEN: [Remains silent, but nods his head and has a faint smile on his face]

COUNSELLOR: Thank you, Ben. Well done ... I notice you are enjoying that experience ... What could we call it?

BEN: [after a long pause]: Confidence .

COUNSELLOR: That's right. You are right ... [matching Ben's pause]. It's confidence ... When you have got as much of that as you need ... you can get really con ... fid ... ent. And as you get really confident in this experience, look even more closely at those leaves on the trees — right into them. And notice, each time you look, there is the face of a different woman ... and on the other side of the leaf you can see yourself ... feeling ... con ... fid ... ent ... and growing in confidence each time you look at the leaves in the forest, feeling comfortable and calm as you see the faces of different women in the leaves ... You can do that now ... maybe ten times, maybe a hundred times, or a thousand, as you count the leaves on the trees ... That's good, Ben ... really good ... Stay with that as long as you can enjoy it ... Each time ... you do it ... *you* know how not to blush.

Case Analysis

Ben showed the counsellor that he was a student and that he used visual–kinaesthetic sensory representations to map out his experience. The student introduced the idea of his blushing being like a traffic light and the counsellor noticed this and extended the metaphor of a sequence being involved in the way Ben created the experience of blushing and anxiety. Ben agreed and rapport began to strengthen between counsellor and client from this point. Ben revealed that he engages in an internal auditory representation of what he sees by saying to himself, "I fancy her", or words to that effect. Immediately after this he experiences blushing and embarrassment. The counsellor congratulated Ben, showing that he knew how to produce his blushing, and linked this to demonstrating that Ben knew how to stop himself from blushing. This part of the session laid the basis for the building of anchors that produced a positive experience associated with good feelings and internal visual representations of a forest and the associations of trees, leaves and birdsong. Ben also had an internal auditory representation in this experience. Linguistically he gave the particular experience of the colours and the sounds and the accompanying kinaesthetic experience of the forest the name 'confidence'.

The NLP counsellor then re-anchored Ben's experience of seeing women he 'fancied' to the leaves in the forest by embedding the faces of the women in the leaves. As he did this the counsellor utilized the knowledge that Ben was a student and invited him to 'really study' the leaves and told him that each time he did so he could grow in confidence. The session concluded with the NLP counsellor providing feedback to Ben that he knew how not to blush and to feel really good as he repeated the experience over and over again.

Case Example Three: Collapsing Anchors

Frequently clients come to counselling saying they are suffering from fear and anxiety. It can be fear or anxiety about many situations or one particular kind of situation. Fear and anxiety can be such a crippling experience for many clients that it can prevent them from living a purposeful or satisfying life.

Mary, aged 47, came to the counselling clinic saying she had a terrible fear of failure. The counsellor talked to her about the many fears that people have and mentioned that he used to feel quite anxious and fearful each time he met a new person. Mary gave him permission to touch her hands during the session, as he explained that this was part of the method they would be using during their sessions together.

She agreed to complete a personal fear inventory. The counsellor said she could concentrate when she was ready to concentrate and she could think long and hard about the situations she found fearful and about those in which she was anxious. As they worked together, Mary found that she had a very pronounced fear of failure. Here is a part of the session on collapsing anchors carried out by the NLP counsellor. Pay attention to the way he worked with Mary. What do you observe?

COUNSELLOR: Mary, thanks for agreeing to complete the test on the Fear Survey Inventory.
MARY: That's all right ... it might help me focus on my problems.
COUNSELLOR: That's right ... we agreed that we would look at the results and see what we make of them ... Is that right?
MARY: Yes, that is right ... I know I came out very fearful and anxious about failure.
COUNSELLOR: Yes, you are correct, Mary. You came out clearly showing you can be very fearful about failure.
MARY: 'Can be'? I'm *always* very fearful about failure.
COUNSELLOR: Always? What are you feeling right now?
MARY: What do you mean? I ...

COUNSELLOR: You are feeling something right now ... Is that correct, Mary?

MARY: Yes, I am ... I'm a bit uhmmm ...

COUNSELLOR: Yes?

MARY: You have upset me ...

COUNSELLOR: And you feel ...

MARY: Disappointed ...

COUNSELLOR: Disappointed?

MARY: Well, more annoyed [*displaying a changed state*] ...

COUNSELLOR: Could you allow that feeling to just get that little bit more intense and annoyed?

MARY: I could, but I would just get angry and lose control.

COUNSELLOR: So being angry means losing control. Is that correct?

MARY: Correct.

COUNSELLOR: You are correct.

MARY: Mmm ... mmm.

COUNSELLOR: Could you lose control right *now*? Right this minute?

MARY: No, I couldn't possibly do that ...

COUNSELLOR: So you can be angry and in control?

MARY: I can ...

COUNSELLOR: That is correct, Mary. *You can ... be in control.* So you can just get a more vivid and colourful picture of yourself being angry and in control ... can you do that? Just take your time ...

MARY: Yes. I have still got the feeling and it's changing now ... uhmm [*her state changes again*] ...

COUNSELLOR: That is good ... What are you getting now?

MARY: There are some pictures, more like the like old black and white snapshots from a holiday I had as a little girl ... I got angry with my little sister ... She really annoyed me ... the little squirt ...

COUNSELLOR: Keep with those pictures. That's right, Mary. Now how can you make them so they are in colour, like the colours of the rainbow? See what you can do ... with them ... and bring them really close to you ... What colours are they now?

MARY: Oh ... I have got red and orange and black and a sort of blue colour, more like the blue you get on a nice sunny day ...

COUNSELLOR: Like a nice sunny day. That is very good ... So

when you have intensified that to your liking, tell me ... what shall we call that experience?

MARY: *Control.*

COUNSELLOR: *Control*: that is correct, Mary. I would like to ask you which hand you can use that we can say is your *control*.

MARY: Funnily enough, I want to say my left hand.

COUNSELLOR: That is OK, Mary. You can say it, if you want to.

MARY: My left hand is *control.*

COUNSELLOR: OK, Mary. When I touch your hand like this [*he lightly touches the palm of her left hand*] you say to yourself ...

MARY: *Control.*

COUNSELLOR: And you get the colour and the pictures and the nearness and brightness. You make all of that control ... have you got it?

MARY: Mmm. Yes, I have [*her state changes again*] *I have control.*

COUNSELLOR: That is correct, Mary ... *You* have control ... Now how does that feel?

MARY: Great. Honest, really great. I can see myself just like that day.

COUNSELLOR: OK. You have done really well, Mary. Let us just do the *control* thing again several times. I touch your hand lightly, like this and ...

MARY: I get the pictures again and I have got, and I can hear myself saying, *control* ... mmm ... yeh.

COUNSELLOR: Great, Mary. When you run it past yourself and see it clearly and get the feelings and you say *control*, come away from that experience ... Just come away. You can go back there any time you want now ... Isn't that right?

MARY: Mmm ... that's right. That's right ...

COUNSELLOR: Now come to your right hand and visualize the experience you get when you see yourself being afraid of failure ... What is developing?

MARY: I see myself in my room. I am 12. I have been left there because I failed an exam to get to grammar school ... It is a horrible place now ... all alone ... scared ... really scared.

COUNSELLOR: You are very frightened in this room, so can you make the room so dim it is not easy to see which room it is and sit here with me safe and look back at the dim room ... and what do you see now?

MARY: Just an outline of myself.

COUNSELLOR: Now that outline, Mary, make sure it is at a safe enough distance from you and smaller and tinier and vague ... that's right, make it vague ...

MARY: It is difficult ...

COUNSELLOR: Yes ... difficult ... What is the first bit you can change?

MARY: The size. I can do that ... I can make it smaller.

COUNSELLOR: OK. Make it smaller first and then further away and more vague ... Take your time. You can control it.

MARY: Mmm ... Yes, I have got it under control now. It is smaller, a bit further away and still there, but definitely more vague.

COUNSELLOR: That is very good. Run it past yourself quite a few times, until you are satisfied with it.

MARY: Yes ... That's fine now ...

COUNSELLOR: What shall we call this one, Mary?

MARY: This one is easier ... I will call it 'The Room'.

COUNSELLOR: So when I touch your right hand you get 'The Room' experience. Is that right, Mary?

MARY: Yes, I get it, but a bit smaller and further away than before and less clear ... That is it ...

COUNSELLOR: OK, Mary. So as I touch your left hand like this there are times when ... you can have this experience — the experience of *control* — and as I touch the other one you get 'The Room' ...

MARY: Mmm ... I do ... first one, then the other ...

COUNSELLOR: That is very good, Mary ... Now, as I touch both your hands at the same time, like this, notice what happens [*he touches her left and right palms at the same time*].

MARY: Hmm ... All ... er ... mixed up ... Yes, mixed up.

COUNSELLOR: That's good. That is really very good, Mary. Now just take that a bit further and you can be curious about what happens next as I do this with your hands [*he keeps touching both palms, but applies more pressure on the left and lightens the touch on the right and then stops touching the right hand and keeps touching the palm of the left hand*]. You have control ... What is happening now, Mary?

MARY: It feels better ... a lot better ...

COUNSELLOR: OK. You can see how you have passed into control. Stay with that and let's take your control into a specific situation and you can be safe and test it ... Would you like to do that now?

MARY: Mmm ... I would like that ...

Analysis

In collapsing anchors the NLP counsellor had a clear outcome in mind. The anchor that produced unpleasant or unwanted experiences for Mary had to be lifted or give way to a more powerful anchor that replaced or neutralized it. In Mary's case, she had a fear of failure and was anchored to an unwanted experience connected with an exam result and 'The Room.' The counsellor was able to help Mary gain access to a state where she felt much more resourceful and this was then anchored to a state she described as 'control'. Notice how the resourceful state was set up *first* and firmly established with Mary before they moved on to calling up the fear of failure and the state anchored to 'The Room'. A subtle and important opening was made to the session by the NLP counsellor framing the session as one where Mary had agreed to 'complete a test': he began the session by linguistically framing it as one where Mary had already begun to overcome her fear of failure.

At other times during the counselling session the counsellor repeatedly told Mary, "You are correct", "That is right" and that Mary had 'passed' into control. The counsellor drew attention to the present time as a way of getting her to experience the fact that she does not always feel fearful in 'testing' situations. As the session continued, Mary found that she could have another emotion — anger — and yet still be in control of herself. The theme of control was then anchored securely to Mary. The NLP counsellor used the upturned palms of Mary's hands to set up the anchors and then collapse them. It was also noticeable that the counsellor asked Mary which hands would be used for the different anchors and what they should be called. All of this approach to re-anchoring implied that Mary had control: the very experience that she wished to have and the resource state she required to collapse the unwanted anchor of 'The Room'.

In the closing stages of the counselling session the counsellor set up future pacing with Mary. The scene was set for rehearsal and safe 'testing' of the control she now had in specific situations. The anchors had been collapsed and she was now in a more personally resourceful state. She felt more in control and ready to face the future.

Personal Outcomes
●

Despite often being anchored to habits, each time a client comes to counselling, they are doing the best they can. They are consciously or unconsciously working on personal outcomes they want to experience in their lives. Most of the time this works. Clients make the choices they think are readily available to them.

A person wants to experience the feelings of excitement, fear and compassion in a safe way. So what do they do? They buy a video and give themselves the experience in their own home. They accomplish their personal outcome. They do it in a way that is acceptable to them. Each day millions of people are engaging in producing personal outcomes for themselves. Some they like; some they can tolerate; some they choose but, ironically, do not want in their lives at any price. However, whatever they do, the basic principle is the same. They are engaging in different ways of representing their realities and engaging in personal strategies. These result in outcomes that give them experiences they want or do not want, or are unsure whether they want or not; or they have experiences which they want more or less of in the future.

As we have seen throughout this book, clients often end up coming to counselling because they want to experience different personal outcomes. They have not yet found other ways of changing their representations of external environments or small or large parts of themselves that will give them the experiences they desire. One result of this is that people sometimes suffer great distress and psychological and physical pain. The distress, discomfort, pain, anxiety, depression and anger, the disturbing circumstances in which clients may find themselves — these are all real enough, but they should not be confused with the real problem. From an NLP perspective on counselling, the central problem of clients is clear: *they have not yet created a personal strategy that will most effectively and efficiently secure a particular outcome they want to experience.*

For William Glasser, the founder of reality therapy, the difficulty clients faced was one of acting irresponsibly and not fulfilling their needs. For the NLP counsellor, stress, sickness and psychological problems come about because clients have yet to change and choose a different personal strategy. When clients can do this, they can have different experiences. The first step in making changes and creating new choices is helping the client to be clear about what they want and do not want and with whom, and how they will know when they have realized a particular personal outcome.

NLP Counselling and Well Formed Outcomes

How this is done is unique to each client and counsellor. However the task for the NLP counsellor is the same for each client. They work towards the creation of *well formed outcomes*. This can happen at any point during the counselling process. Some clients are logical, think sequentially and have simple, easily resolvable, problems. They know what they want; they know how they wish to experience what they want and with whom, where and when. With these clients the NLP counsellor can begin to identify well formed outcomes within the first few sessions of counselling.

Conversely many clients are not sure about the outcomes they wish to experience. These clients may often arrive for counselling in emotionally charged states. They find it difficult to be rational and object to a mechanical or systematic and methodical approach to identifying and creating well formed outcomes. We believe it is up to the NLP counsellor to calibrate the readiness of clients to work on personal outcomes and to make these relevant and well formed with clients.

Although the creation of well formed outcomes in NLP is unique to each client, clients share in a common process.

Changing from a Present State to a Desired Future State

First the counsellor needs to check with clients that they really do want to move from their present state to a desired future state. Some clients would rather hold on to the hell they experience than give it up. Or they fear that giving up the present state would lead to a much more undesirable state and are not motivated to change. On other occasions clients obtain secondary gain from remaining in their present state. For example, being ill is unpleasant but it generates sympathy and concern from important people in the client's life.

Stating in Positives

When well formed outcomes are being developed with clients they need to be created in a way that can be stated positively. Most clients in counselling will be able to tell you what they do not want. It is essential in NLP counselling for clients to be able to say what they do want and what having the new outcome or experience will do for them. The NLP counsellor therefore needs to be able to explore with clients such questions as the following:

▶ What do you really want?
▶ What would you rather have than what you have now?
▶ How do you know when you know what you want?
▶ What will having what you want do for you?
▶ What small change would you like to see/feel/tune in to now?
▶ How can you start to understand what you want?
▶ What would you like to be attainable for you at this time?
▶ How could you know what you really wanted?
▶ Think of a time when you really knew what you wanted: what did you experience?
▶ How in the past have you experienced something you really wanted?
▶ Pick a specific event or occasion when you have experienced knowing what you want and ask yourself how you knew it.
▶ Ask yourself right now what you know about what you want from your situation.

► Taking everything we have talked about into consideration, tell me what you want.

► How do you know what you want?

► How would I know that what you want is what you wanted to experience as an outcome for yourself?

'Owning' Outcomes

As with other forms of counselling, the NLP counselling process works best when the client 'owns' the outcome she wants to experience in a desired state. It is of little use for counsellors to force upon clients the outcomes they believe clients should have, unless clients really want it that way. The point about owning outcomes is to ensure that clients really want them. One way of testing this in counselling sessions with NLP is to find out what the client can and will do that is within their control to start to bring their outcome or desired state about. In this case the NLP counsellor asks such questions as the following:

► How much do you *want* this outcome?

► What could you start to change?

► Would you start by making a big or a small change?

► What can you be doing *now* to reach your outcome?

► How would you begin to do something about moving towards your outcome?

► How can you keep committed to achieving your outcome?

► Where will/would you start?

► When will/would you start?

► How will you know when you have made a start?

► How will I know?

Specifying and Sensory Experience

Once clients know what they want and are committed to change and attaining their personal outcomes, the NLP counsellor will often work with them to specify more precisely what they want and how it will be represented in their experience. To say this is not to contradict use of the nominalizations of clients to help them change and choose new strategies for experiencing their world.

However, in many cases, clients need to become much more specific about the outcomes they want and it is the responsibility of the NLP counsellor to create conditions in the counselling sessions where this can take place. The questions the NLP counsellor uses in counselling to help clients be more specific may include the following:

▶ Where do you want to experience this outcome?
▶ Who else should be part of it?
▶ When will you want it to happen?
▶ How do you intend to experience this outcome?
▶ How much/little do you want?
▶ How specifically will you/won't you ...?
▶ When specifically will you/won't you ...?
▶ What specifically will you/won't you ...?
▶ Where specifically do you ...?
▶ What will be the specific experience you will be ...?
▶ Who specifically will you ...?
▶ When you think of your outcome, what is the way you would specifically see it/feel it/listen for it?
▶ How then, to be more exact, will you know when you ...?
▶ How then, to be more exact, will I know when you ...?
▶ What then, to be more exact, will the difference be that ...?
▶ Which specific week/day/hour/time will you ...?
▶ Which person will you start doing this with first?
▶ At which point will you say ...?
▶ Where exactly will you look?
▶ What words will you actually use when you speak to ...?
▶ The next time you hear him/her say that, what in particular will you say in reply?
▶ When he/she looks at you like that again, what is the particular look you will have on your face?
▶ Would you show me/tell me exactly how you will go about it.

Evidence Testing

At different points in counselling with NLP, the counsellor needs to agree, clarify and confirm what will count as evidence that clients are moving towards, moving away from, or achieving their outcomes. The significance of the evidence of change for clients may differ for each person in counselling. However the NLP counsellor can adopt a range of questioning skills which are applicable across a very wide range of problems and client concerns.

With these, the NLP counsellor can assess, test and establish client evidence and the significance it has for them. Thus we have *evidence* and *significance* as two practical guidelines to follow when testing for evidence of change in the present state and desired states of clients. The NLP counsellor should therefore work with clients on the kinds of questions that elicit this personal information. Such questions may include the following:

▶ When will you see when you have your outcome?
▶ When will others see when you have it?
▶ Where will they see it?
▶ What will be different?
▶ How much do you want it: not very much, a little, quite a lot, a great deal?
▶ What tells you that you really want this outcome?
▶ How many hours/days/weeks/months/ should it take to reach your outcome?
▶ What will you feel when you have your outcome?
▶ Could you be clearer about what you will be picturing in your mind ?
▶ What will you be saying to yourself?
▶ What will other people see/feel/hear/say?
▶ How will you know it is what you want?
▶ What would stop you from getting what you want?
▶ What would stop you from maintaining what you get?
▶ What would stop you transferring what you get into your ...?
▶ How will doing it that way help you get ...?
▶ What is it about thinking in that way that will help you get what you want?
▶ You can do it that way; so how much does it mean to you?
▶ You can see it that way; so how right does it look?
▶ You can talk about it to him/her like that; so how right does that sound to you?

► You can feel it like that; so how much can you trust that feeling?

► You can do it/see it/feel it/talk about it like that; so will it give you the experience you want?

► If you do it/see it/feel it/talk about it like that, what, to be more exact, would the outcome be for you?

Ecological Checking

It is equally important to check with clients the ecological consequences of their personal outcomes. Well formed outcomes also rely on clients being satisfied with the consequences for themselves and their relationships if they were to achieve their sought outcome. Ecological checking — the mapping of the way client outcomes are likely to affect themselves and others in the present and the future — is fundamental to NLP counselling. As in other forms of counselling, NLP counsellors are not simply interested in clients changing for the sake of change. The criteria for ecological checking are (1) being sure enough that clients want the outcome they say they want to experience; (2) acquiring sufficient client information upon which they can choose to change or not to change; and (3) having a basis upon which clients can choose a different strategy that may or may not affect their other relationships. The types of questions asked include the following:

► What do you get from what you do now?
► What would you have to give up to get what you want?
► What would you lose by getting what you want?
► Who else would be affected by your outcome?
► Who else would gain from your getting what you want?
► What specifically would they gain?
► Who else would lose?
► What would they lose?
► Where/in which other situations do you want this change?
► Who else do you want to share in this change?
► How could you change your outcome to take these others into consideration?

▶ How far will making this change be worthwhile for you/for others?

▶ What degree of willingness have you got to make this change/ these changes?

▶ When you consider it, how close are these changes to what you want?

▶ What will this change/these changes mean to you?

▶ What might you want to alter before you make your change/changes?

Resourcing Action for Change

Clearly NLP counsellors have a responsibility to make explicit the outcomes that clients wish to choose and change in their lives. These, and how clients want to experience them, have to be identified and specified. We also need to be satisfied that clients have access to sufficient significant resources to initiate the actions that lead to change.

There are many aspects of resourcing action that will lead to change for clients in NLP counselling. Some of the main questions that can be covered with clients can be stated. For the most part, the NLP counsellor asks questions which elicit states whereby the client feels resourceful or recalls being resourceful and able to change. Typical questions include the following:

▶ What do you need to bring about the changes you have just talked about?

▶ What do you see would provide a clear picture of the way you can bring these changes about?

▶ If you think of a time when you managed to do something that was difficult and you overcame a problem, how did you manage to do that?

▶ If you get a clear picture in your mind — a snapshot of yourself when you got something into perspective and made a change in your life — what happens when we turn that into a movie and make the changes as you think about or recall it?

▶ If you are curious and listen to that inner voice you have been talking about, ask it now how it managed to help you in the past/what it did for you and what it says to you today.

▶ Can you locate that feeling of knowing you are right and that gut-feeling of confidence? Stay with that for a few moments ... now what does it give you – about how you can deal with your present concern?

▶ If you represent the feeling of being in charge, bring it into your present situation and just let that feeling grow, what happens?

▶ You say you can see where you put light on your situation in the past. Just be interested in asking yourself this question: could you see where you can put some light on your situation, and can you imagine for a moment how to create a more positive impression that can lead into new developments?

▶ If you listen very carefully to yourself guiding you through the next steps to a solution, what are you saying you can do today/tomorrow/next week?

▶ Rehearsing how you will do this in your mind right now, ask yourself: how will I say it/see it/feel it when I ...?

▶ Notice where you will be like this and how different it will be.

Choosing Personal Outcomes and Desired States

The main thrust of NLP counselling with clients is to enlarge the variety, type and range of choices they can call up, and make available to themselves. When we can do this, clients can increase the probability of knowing the personal outcomes they want for themselves. They can free themselves from habits they are anchored to and which have held them back or continue to hold them down. They can choose to have different experiences. Sensitive questioning, with appropriate rapport, helps clients to choose what they want. It also helps them to know what they do not want to choose. Of particular importance, counselling with NLP enables clients to make new choices and have the experiences they want but previously believed were inaccessible to them, because the process of counselling with NLP is guided by a fundamental assumption: clients already have latent within themselves all of the potential resources to experience the states they desire in their lives.

Our purpose as counsellors using NLP in counselling is therefore strikingly clear. We work with clients to make new choices available and accessible to them in order that they can choose to change some aspect of the way they represent their experience.

Chapter 10

THE UTILIZATION
PRINCIPLE

NLP Techniques and Beyond

●

As you may have noticed throughout this book, many techniques play a valuable and central part in counselling with NLP. We have emphasized how different ways of modelling reality and creating new choices for clients can lead to the personal outcomes they wish to experience in their lives.

The NLP techniques we have illustrated and exemplified here are all part of an even more extensive range of counselling methods and approaches that support the practice of NLP counselling. What are the main contributions NLP techniques make towards counselling clients? They help counsellors to create, maintain and break rapport with clients. They make it possible to gain access to and gather significant personal information and create new choices that change the pattern of client thinking, feeling and behaviour. In NLP terms, NLP provides counsellors with a technology to empower clients so they can move from their present state to more desired states.

Underlying these NLP techniques which undoubtedly help counsellors to help their clients change is a fundamental assumption: each person is an individual. NLP counselling works best when it is shaped to each individual, their sensory–cognitive and linguistic map of reality. Therefore it is worth regularly reminding ourselves that NLP counselling is adapted to individuals rather than individuals being given a standard NLP technique to 'solve their problems'. Another way of putting this point is that counsellors using NLP are not technique-driven. Being vigilant about this increases the probability that clients will be able to change, should they wish to, and realize their personal outcomes and not those of the counsellor.

Counsellors who use NLP in their counselling may utilize the technology of NLP to enable the client to change, but the agenda for change belongs to the client. NLP counselling is a client-based activity. NLP counselling must therefore go beyond the mindless application of NLP techniques. Counsellors who rely on the blind deployment of NLP techniques are trying to paint by numbers in the hope of producing a worthwhile piece of original art.

The main task for counsellors working with clients is to be flexible enough in their practice to create the climate in counselling where client change can take place. Quite simply we need to be innovative in our efforts at helping people change. How we go about this spontaneously informs the strategy and direction counselling and therapy will take with each client. Utilization is the core concept of NLP that makes it possible to go beyond mere deployment of NLP techniques in counselling clients. It is a principle that makes NLP counselling different from other forms of counselling.

The practice of NLP counselling is replete with innovative and creative examples of utilization in action, but one example must suffice here.

Utilization in Action: a Client Example

●

Marlene, a 13-year-old, came to counselling with her mother Jen. Jen reported that Marlene was suffering from a severe lack of confidence. Utilizing the idea of confidence the counsellor worked with Marlene and Jen. Within two NLP counselling sessions some significant improvements were made.

At the first session, Jen went through a vast catalogue of things that Marlene could not do at home or at school and how this worried Jen. In Marlene's presence, Jen also spent some time going into detail about the fact that Marlene did not have any friends and how life was made impossible for Jen at times with Marlene because she was 'like a limpet', so 'clingy' to Jen and too much of a baby for a 13-year old.

During these accounts of Marlene's 'problems', Marlene hung her head and kept her hair over her face so Jen and the counsellors could not see her expression. At one point Marlene looked up for an instant. She was crying. Jen ended by stating it was confidence Marlene lacked; she had tried everything to help her and nothing had worked. Here is what the counsellor did.

He hung his head at about the same angle as Marlene, looking at her and saying to Jen in a weepy voice, "You are absolutely right, Jen. Everything you have done has not worked. Reminding Marlene about how she lacks confidence does not work. It simply acts to further undermine her already poor self-esteem." Jen said that was Marlene showing how she did not believe in herself and was getting all weepy again and that she hung her head like that all the time. The NLP counsellor then said, "Marlene, you are hanging your head. Is that right?" Marlene did not reply, but just nodded.

The counsellor then turned to Jen, raising his head a little, and said, "Everyone knows that people who hang their head are good at thinking. Have you ever seen or heard of that great piece of sculpture — what is it called again?" Jen said " 'The Thinker' " and at that point Marlene looked up a little at her mother. And the counsellor said, "That's right, 'The Thinker'. And you know the Thinker lowered his head when there was a lot of thinking to be done, and maybe you realize you have to do some thinking for yourself."

The counsellor then asked Jen, "What do you think of that?" Jen said, "I have never thought of it like that before." The counsellor asked her to think about it now and said that everyone knew that when someone lowered their head they were thinking people: "People who are thinking lower their head and are considerate, conscientious and concentrating on what is being said and that means they are listening to what has to be done ..." The counsellor looked down and round towards Marlene and said to Jen, while looking at Marlene, "Look. Marlene is thinking. Isn't that right, Marlene?" Marlene nodded her head and whispered that yes, she was thinking.

This session went ahead with nine practical tasks being identified that Marlene and Jen would be able to carry out. Near the end of the first session, the counsellor thanked Marlene and

Jen for coming to their first session but said there seemed to be something missing. He asked Marlene and Jen, "Can you imagine what it is? Go on, have a guess." Both Marlene and Jen said they did not know what was missing. Marlene then said, "Maybe it's confidence." The counsellor said, "Sometimes we don't know what is missing and thinking about it can be one way to discover it ... and your thinking tells you it could be con ... fidence. Yes, con ... fidence. That is right, con ... fidence ... [*emphasizing the 'con', so it could be heard as a separate word on its own*]. Well, that is good, because we know that Marlene you already know how to do con ... fidence; you can do con ... siderate, and you can do con ... scientious .... and you can do con ... centration ... These are all things you can do ... And Jen, you notice that, do you? That Marlene can do ... con ... fidence?"

"Yes I do ... now you mention it ..."

"You can?"

"Yes, I can, I really can."

"Yes, you can ... So I wonder if I could ask you both something right now ... When you add the fingers you have on your left and right hands, how many fingers does that make for you?" Marlene and Jen said "ten" almost at the same time. "Yes, ten," agreed the counsellor. "So we have nine tasks. One is missing and when you find the missing one it will make ten. Just like the ten fingers on your hands. You are confident you have ten fingers on your hands, is that right?" Both Marlene and Jen nodded vigorously and said "yes" and the counsellor said, "So you know what you have got on your hands — the answer is right there on your finger tips and I would like to give you a clue about finding the tenth task ... Here it is: there is something that you can do, Marlene, that Mum cannot do. I would like you to take your time and be con ... siderate. Now just be conscientious enough to take time to concentrate on what it is ... I would like you to do that now ... Think about it." Silence followed and Jen and Marlene exchanged smiles and glances. Then Marlene whispered something and the counsellor leaned over and said Marlene could whisper more quietly if she wanted to or more loudly if she wanted Jen to hear. Marlene said in a louder voice, "Mummy is frightened of the water ... I can swim and she can't swim." The counsellor asked Jen and Marlene again if that was right and they agreed and Jen went into a long description of how she was not confident enough to swim. Jen, turning and looking at Marlene, said buoyantly, "Oh, Marlene is very confident — aren't you, Marlene? In swimming she is as happy as a fish in water." The counsellor thanked Jen and Marlene for identifying the tenth task, the one that was to be added to the other nine to make ten. It was clear and simple: Marlene would teach her mother Jen how to get over the fear of swimming. The session ended with Marlene and Jen agreeing to carry out their tasks and bring back their experience of doing so to their next counselling session.

As this case shows, utilization is what makes counselling with NLP different from other forms of counselling. The counsellor utilized the client's frame of reference. NLP counsellors work at understanding the personal maps of clients and the territory they represent, and the particular ways in which the representation of each person's reality is constructed. Everyone is different. No two people are the same and no one person is the same across all situations. Even if they were, it is not the NLP counsellor's job to decide for the client but rather to explore the terrain of the territory that the personal maps of clients hold as their current reality. In time, and within or over sessions, the NLP counsellor helps the client to re-anchor, reframe or use other methods of change such as story-telling or metaphor in the reconstruction of their realities. Doing this makes the mission of NLP counselling clear: creating the conditions in counselling whereby clients can change from the states they currently experience to more desired states.

Utilization provides the counsellor with the possibilities of the present. These unique possibilities are to be found in each client within each counselling session. Clearly NLP counselling of itself cannot and will not create client change, but the counsellor needs to appreciate the essential and unique importance of utilization and the difference it can make to the enterprise of NLP counselling, and so strengthen the range, depth and quality of help they offer their clients.

GLOSSARY OF PRINCIPAL TERMS IN NLP COUNSELLING

Accessing cues The behaviours engaged in by clients: breathing, eye movements, posture, gestures and linguistic patterns that serve to indicate how they are processing information internally

Analogical principle The process of continuous variability used with clients between limits involving 'more or less' representations: a dimmer light switch is a good example of the analogical principle

Anchoring The process by which any external stimulus or internal representation is, or becomes, associated with, and triggers an internal response that is rapidly retrieved (similar to classical conditioning)

'As if' frame A technique whereby clients can engage in assuming that an event has already taken place in order to facilitate creative problem solving and overcome self-imposed limitations

Associated state The re-experiencing of feelings and emotions and the sights, sounds, tastes and smells of an event without it necessarily occurring in the present

Attention   The intentional and selective focusing of awareness

Auditory   Concerned with the representation of hearing

Behaviour   Any activity engaged in by clients, including their sensory and cognitive representations, language and thinking

Behavioural flexibility   The ability of clients to vary their behaviour in order to obtain a particular response from another person

Beliefs   Generalizations made up about the world that inform and guide specific behaviours

Calibration   Ability to notice and accurately assess client states and changes in their states based on their non-verbal behaviour

Capability   The degree to which a client has patterned a successful strategy for carrying out a task

Change   The differences that occur in the sensory representations, cognitive and linguistic maps and the states of clients; expressed as behaviour

Chunking   The process of changing perceptions by moving up or down logical levels. Chunking up means going towards generalizations and whole classes, including the members in that class. Chunking down involves moving down towards specific members of a class or parts of the whole. An example of chunking up would be talking about a personal relationship and the place of conflict and aggression in it. In chunking down we could ask for a specific example or detailed recent episode where conflict and aggression were present in the relationship

Congruity	A situation where the different modalities used by a client are the same or similar to the expression she gives to her experience. For instance, the alignment of tone of voice, the words said and the meaning of what they say: a client has tears in her eyes, and in a tremulous voice says she is sorry for her actions or what she did to another person
Conscious	Anything in the present moment of her experience of which a client is aware
Control	The process a client uses to retain their integrity, identity and performance in the midst of changing circumstances
Criterion	What is significant to the client in any specific context or situation
Crossover mirroring	Matching client movements with different ones: for example, blinking your eyes in rhythm with their breathing
Deep structure	The conscious and unconscious sensory, cognitive and linguistic maps that clients use to organize, guide and direct their behaviour
Deletion	Intentional or unintentional omission of aspects of experience that have no internal representation by clients. This process helps clients to manage their world and avoid them being overcome by waves of unwanted stimulation. However it can also mean leaving out things that need to be included in their lives
Digital processing	The process of absolute polarity used with clients between limits involving 'all or none' representations: the on/off light switch is a practical example of the digital principle

Distortion   Intentionally or unintentionally inaccurate inclusion of aspects of experience in a client's internal representation in some way that limits them. Two client examples could be a 'warped way of looking at it' or 'only hearing the bad news'

Dovetailing   A situation where the process of fitting two different outcomes together results in a joint solution

Downtime   The state where sensory awareness and processes of attention are directed internally and towards inner sensations, thoughts, memories and feelings

Ecology   The complete set of relationships between a person and their environment; extending to inclusion of the internal ecology and patterns of values, thoughts, feelings, strategies and behaviours a person embodies in relationship to themselves

Elicitation   The procedure used to gather information in an ordered way so that it can be made explicit what behaviour evokes a particular state in a client

Eye accessing   The specific eye movements that are indicative of types of thinking correlated with visual, auditory and kinaesthetic processes

Feedback   Reviewing and summarizing client states, through the use of clients' non-verbal behaviour, language, structure, content and tonality

Frame   The context or circumstances established whereby a past, present or future event is perceived in a particular way

Future pace   The process of mentally rehearsing an outcome to ensure that the desired behaviour will occur elegantly and automatically in a future situation

Generalization   Intentional or unintentional representation of aspects of experience as a whole class of that experience without access being had to the complete class of experiences that is being referred to. A helpful generalization would be: 'Don't put your hands on a hot oven'; an unhelpful generalization would be: 'Flying will kill you'

Gustatory   To do with experiences and representations made by the processes associated with taste

Internal representation   The configurations of hot and cold information created, accommodated and assimilated, stored and recalled in the mind of clients in the form of language, images, sounds, feelings, smells and tastes. For example, asking a client to recall the day they were married requires them to make an internal representation of that day

Kinaesthetic   To do with those experiences and representations made through the processes associated with feelings, the tactile sense and perception of emotions

Lead system   The particular sensory-representational system in use that seeks and provides information to consciousness

Leading   Changes in counsellor behaviour that continue to maintain sufficient rapport for the client to follow

Logical levels   The different logical levels used by clients to order and make sense of their experience

Map	The composite way in which a client structures information and represents the configuration in her personal reality
Matching	Adopting pieces of client behaviour with the intention of enhancing rapport
Meta-model	Representations of a representation of reality such as sensory systems and deletion, distortion and generalization and language are representations of the experience of the client through the senses, predicates, meanings and metaphors
Metaphor	A universal way of using descriptions, enaction, or making reference to, or for, one or more things to describe them because of some similarity between them or their field of relations
Mirroring	Adopting pieces or sequences of client behaviour and behaving as if you were a mirror image of their behaviour. For example, if a client tapped the index finger of her left hand, the counsellor could use mirroring by tapping the index finger of his right hand
Modelling	The process of identifying and selectively patterning those sequences of representations and behaviours that lead a client to accomplish a task
Neurolinguistic programming	The study of the structure of subjective experience and human excellence
Nominalization	Unspecified linguistic term used by clients involved in the process of transforming verbs into nouns and using them as if they denoted a concrete entity. An example of a nominalization would be someone saying they 'are frustrated'

Olfactory	To do with experiences and representations made through the processes associated with smell
Outcome	The results of desired states that clients aspire to realize
Pacing	Obtaining and maintaining rapport with a client through language, behaviour, beliefs, moods, values and interests that match their model of the world
Perceptual filters	The cognitions, beliefs, experiences and language that clients use in the formation of their model of the world and to underpin their personal map of reality
Predicates	Words used in descriptions by clients that are indicative of a specific sensory representational system: eg. a clear view/sounds like a clash/ weight of the world on my shoulders/smell of fear/leaves a bad taste in the mouth
Preferred system	The most frequent representational system typically used by clients to construct or retrieve information and organize their experience
Reframing	A way of changing the reference orientation of clients in order that they experience a different meaning for the same referent
Reframing by content	Changing the experience a client has by taking a statement and creating a different meaning: eg. "What else could this mean?"; "It could also mean ..."
Reframing by context	Changing the experience a client has by creating a different meaning for the same situation: eg. "Where would this behaviour be OK?"

Representational system	The processing system used by clients to engage a particular sensory modality at any one moment in time and over time to code, store and retrieve personal information
Sensory acuity	The senses used at any particular time to make distinctions about the world
Sensory description	Conveying information that is directly observable and verifiable through the senses. Compare "His lips are curled up and four teeth are showing; the eyes are slightly closed" with "He is happy". The first description is sensory based. The second is a value judgement based on interpretation of what has been observed
State	The sum total of all sensory–perceptual and psycho-neurolinguistic processes that give rise to mood and the way a client feels at any one time
Strategy	A known or unknown systematic and ordered sequence of cognition and behaviour, leading to a specific outcome. A strategy usually includes, in a particular order, each of the sensory–representational systems
Submodalities	Subclassifications within each sensory system associated with qualities of internal representation such as brightness, distance, position, sound, volume, pitch and tone
Surface structure	Words and linguistic forms that are used to symbolize, describe and express the actual primary sensory representations stored in the brain

Synaesthesia	Processes involved in the overlapping between two representational systems such as those exemplified by 'touch–feel', 'see–feel', 'hear–see', 'see–hear', 'look–feel', whereby clients can get feelings from linking two sensory modalities
Third position	Often used with clients to enable them to perceive a concern from the safe position of a detached and benevolent observer. One of three perceptual positions
Timeline	The way that representations are stored and reconstructed as pictures, sounds and feelings of past, present and future
Unconscious	All that is not included in present-moment awareness
Uptime	The present state where sensory-representational and attentional processes are directed outwards towards the external world
Utilization	Those processes whereby an existing strategy is elicited, enlisted and applied, with the purpose of helping a client accomplish a desired outcome
Well formed outcome	Ways of conceiving and expressing outcomes which make them observable, achievable and verifiable, based on identifiable data and criteria

BIBLIOGRAPHY

Argyle M, *The Psychology of Interpersonal Behaviour*, Penguin Books, Harmondsworth, 1977.

Bailey R, *Practical Counselling Skills*, Winslow Press/Speechmark, Bicester, 1993.

Bailey R & Clarke M, *Stress and Coping in Nursing*, Chapman & Hall, London, 1989.

Bandler R, *Using Your Brain For A Change*, Real People Press, Moab, Utah, 1985.

Bandler R & Grinder J, *Frogs into Princes*, Eden Grove Editions, London, 1990.

Bandler R & Grinder J, *Patterns*, Meta Publications, Cupertino, California, 1975.

Bandler R & Grinder J, *Patterns of the Hypnotic Techniques of Milton Erickson MD*, Meta Publications, Cupertino, California, 1975.

Bandler R & Grinder J, *The Structure of Magic I*, Science Behavior Books, Palo Alto, California, 1975.

Bandler R & Grinder J, *The Structure of Magic II*, Science & Behavior Books, Palo Alto, California, 1976.

Bateson G, *Steps to an Ecology of Mind*, Ballantine Books, New York, 1972.

Blackstone J & Josipovic Z (eds), *Zen For Beginners*, Unwin Paperbacks, London, 1986.

Bretto C, *A Framework for Excellence*, Capitola, California, 1988.

Castaneda C, *A Separate Reality*, Penguin, Harmondsworth, 1985.

Erickson M & Rossi E, *Hypnotic Realities*, Irvington Publishers Inc, New York, 1976.

Erickson M & Rossi E, *Hypnotherapy*, Irvington Publishers Inc, New York, 1992.

Glasser W, *Reality Therapy*, Harper & Row, New York, 1975.

Glasser W, *Stations of the Mind*, Harper & Row, New York, 1981.

Glasser W, *Control Theory*, Harper & Row, New York, 1984.

Gordon D, *Therapeutic Metaphors*, Meta Publications, Cupertino, California, 1978.

Greene J, *Psycholinguistics*, Penguin, Harmondsworth, 1972.

Grinder J & Bandler R, *The Structure of Magic II*, Science & Behavior Books, Palo Alto, California, 1976.

Haley J, *Uncommon Therapy*, Norton, New York, 1986.

Huxley A, *The Doors of Perception*, Grafton, HarperCollins, London, 1977.

Keenan B, *An Evil Cradling*, Hutchinson, London, 1992.

Lakoff & Johnson, *Metaphors We Live By,* University of Chicago Press, Chicago, 1980.

Lankton S, *Practical Magic*, Meta Publications, Cupertino, California, 1980.

Lazarus R, *Psychological Stress and the Coping Process*, McGraw-Hill, New York, 1966.

Mills J & Crowley R, *Therapeutic Metaphors for Children and the Child Within*, Brunner-Mezel, New York, 1986.

O'Connor J & Seymour J, *Introducing Neuro-Linguistic Programming*, Crucible, Thorsons Publishing Group, Wellingborough, 1990.

Pirsig R, *Zen and The Art of Motorcycle Maintenance*, Bodley Head, London, 1974.

Redfield J, *The Celestine Prophecy*, Bantam Books, London, 1995.

Rogers C, *A Way of Being*, Houghton Mifflin, Boston, 1980.

Rogers C, *On Becoming a Person*, Constable, London, 1986.

Seigler RS, *Children's Thinking*, Prentice-Hall, Englewood Cliffs, 1991.

Sills C, Fish S & Lapworth P, *Gestalt Counselling*, Winslow Press/Speechmark, Bicester, 1995.

Sternberg R, *Beyond IQ: A triadic theory of human intelligence*, Cambridge University Press, New York, 1985.

Toffler A, *Future Shock*, Pan, London, 1971

Waller RJ, *The Bridges of Madison County*, Mandarin, London, 1993.

Watzlawick P, *The Language of Change*, Norton, New York, 1978.

Wolf S & Goodall H, *Stress and Disease*, C.C. Thomas, Springfield, Illinois, 1968.

Wubbolding R, *Using Reality Therapy*, Harper & Row, New York, 1988.

Helping People Change:
The Essential Counselling Series

These books on different approaches to counselling are of immediate practical benefit to everyone in the 'people business'. Written by experienced counsellors respected in their own field, each reveals a different way in which the user can develop counselling skills with clients.

The series is edited by Dr Roy Bailey, a chartered clinical psychologist, counsellor, psychotherapist, trainer and hypnotherapist.

NLP Counselling
Roy Bailey

This latest edition to the essential *Helping People Change* counselling series is written by an established author, editor and NLP counsellor. This comprehensive handbook will be useful to experienced counsellors and covers the basic theory, rapport, metaphor and technology of NLP counselling. Diagrams, tables and case studies augment the textual explanations.

Transactional Analysis Counselling
Phil Lapworth, Charlotte Sills & Sue Fish

Transactional analysis counselling can be beneficial in a variety of situations, especially those of an organisational, educational and personal nature. This immensely practical guide contains the information required to implement this approach and is also an essential work of reference for the practitioner already using TA.

Practical Counselling Skills
Roy Bailey

The first volume to be published in the series, this book is an accessible and straightforward basic guide to counselling, useful to beginner and practitioner alike. Group leaders and tutors running courses which include any element of counselling will also derive great benefit from this title.

Gestalt Counselling
Charlotte Sills, Sue Fish & Phil Lapworth

Covering both theory and practice this intelligible handbook offers a comprehensive guide to the philosophy and technique of Gestalt counselling for both novice and more experienced counsellors.

For further information or to obtain a free copy of our catalogue, please contact:

Speechmark Publishing Ltd
Telford Road, Bicester, Oxon OX26 4LQ, UK